Collins · *do brilliantly !*

CW00531635

Exam**Practice**

AS Business Studies

Exam practice at its **best**

■ **Stuart Merrills**
■ **Series Editor: Jayne de Courcy**

William Collins' dream of knowledge for all began with the publication of his first book in 1819. A self-educated mill worker, he not only enriched millions of lives, but also founded a flourishing publishing house. Today, staying true to this spirit, Collins books are packed with inspiration, innovation and practical expertise. They place you at the centre of a world of possibility and give you exactly what you need to explore it.

Collins. Do more.

Published by HarperCollins*Publishers* Limited
77–85 Fulham Palace Road
London W6 8JB

> www.**Collins**Education.com
> On-line support for schools and colleges

© HarperCollins*Publishers* Ltd 2005
First published 2002
This revised edition published 2005

10 9 8 7 6 5 4 3 2

ISBN-13 978 0 00 719502 2
ISBN-10 0 00 719502 8

Stuart Merrills asserts his moral right to be identified as the author of this work

British Library Cataloguing in Publication Data
A catalogue record for this publication is available from the British Library

Acknowledgements
With grateful thanks to Dawn for her patience and understanding during this project.

The Author and Publishers would like to thank Richard Thompson for his able assistance with the 'Key points to remember' sections.

The Author and Publishers are grateful to the following for permission to reproduce copyright material:

AQA Specimen examination question (pp.80–81) and AQA pre-issued case study (pp.82–87) are reproduced by permission of the Assessment and Qualifications Alliance. The author is responsible for the answers/ commentaries on the question; they have neither been provided nor approved by the AQA and they may not necessarily constitute the only possible solutions.

Every effort has been made to contact the holders of copyright material, but if any have been inadvertently overlooked, the Publishers will be pleased to make the necessary arrangements at the first opportunity.

Illustrations
Cartoon artwork – Roger Penwill
DTP artwork – Gecko Limited

Photographs
The publishers would like to thank the following for permission to reproduce photographs:
Tony Stone, 26.

Edited by Margaret Shepherd and Philippa Boxer
Production by Katie Butler
Book design by Bob Vickers and Gecko Limited
Printed and bound by Printing Express, Hong Kong

> You might also like to visit:
> www.harpercollins.co.uk
> The book lover's website

Contents

How this book will help you
by Stuart Merrills

Exam practice – how to answer questions better

This book will help you to improve your performance in your AS Business Studies exams.

I have marked many exam papers where students haven't used the knowledge that they have as effectively as they could. This means they don't get the grade they are capable of achieving.

To get a good grade in AS Business Studies, you need a good understanding of the subject matter, an up-to-date awareness of current business issues, good communication skills and good exam technique. Your textbook and teacher will help you develop your knowledge and understanding. This book will help you improve your exam technique, so that you can make the most effective use of what you know.

Each chapter in this book is broken down into four separate parts, aimed at giving you the chance to practise and develop your exam technique. It may also help improve your knowledge as well.

1 Exam Question, Student's Answer and 'How to score full marks'

Each chapter starts with an exam question of the sort you will find on a real AS Business Studies paper, followed by a typical student's answer.

The 'How to score full marks' section shows you where and how the answer could be improved, e.g. by explaining what the question is asking for, from pointing out missing knowledge or discussing technique and approach to developing a good response. This means that when you meet these types of questions in your exams, you will know how to tackle them successfully.

Some of the questions require a more developed response and are worth more marks, so I have provided information on alternative approaches, highlighting useful lines of argument and concentrating on the skills of analysis and evaluation that are needed for high marks.

2 'Don't forget...' boxes

These boxes highlight some of the more common mistakes that I see every year in students' exam papers. These include errors both in knowledge and understanding (such as the application of particular theories) as well as mistakes in exam technique.

These boxes form a quick reference guide to building your exam technique.

3 'Key points to remember'

These are the most important aspects that you need to cover when revising the topic. They give you an overview of each topic area so that you can spot any gaps or weaknesses in your knowledge.

Remember that a book of this size cannot be a comprehensive revision guide – that's what your textbook and class notes are for!

4 Question to try with Examiner's hints, Answer and Comments

Each chapter ends with a question for you to try answering. Don't cheat! Sit down and try to answer it as if you were in an exam. Time yourself – this will help make the practice real. Try to remember all that you've read earlier in the chapter and put it into practice. I have given a couple of 'Examiner's hints' to help you tackle the more difficult aspects of the question.

When you've written your answer, check it through and then turn to the back of the book. There you'll find an answer to the question you've just done. These answers are of a good 'A' grade standard. I have added my 'Examiner's comments' to show you exactly why it is such a good answer.

Compare your answer with the answer given. If you feel yours wasn't as good, note the areas where you feel the answer given was better and re-write your answer to develop your technique and improve your grade.

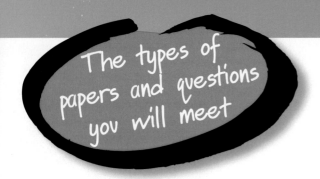
The types of papers and questions you will meet

The most popular exam board for AS Business Studies is AQA. The questions in this book are written mainly for the AQA style of questions. However, the approach used by OCR and Edexcel is similar and all the information on exam technique, the content of answers, the 'Don't forget' boxes, the chapter on how to approach the pre-issued case study and the 'Key points' sections are useful whichever board you are with.

Data-response or stimulus papers

For AQA candidates, paper 1 is a data-response paper and contains two stimulus items. You are given some initial background information that provides a scenario on which the examination questions are set. Each piece of stimulus material has 4–5 questions totalling 25 marks. For OCR paper 2 candidates, the style is similar but the questions total 43 marks. Edexcel also use this style of questions in their modular exam.

The stimulus material may be based on newspaper or magazine extracts, or be entirely fictitious. It may contain data in the form of tables, charts, graphs or diagrams. Remember that the stimulus material is there to help you. In order to gain high marks in this sort of question, you must put your answers in context i.e. respond to the circumstances in the stimulus material given.

Case study paper

All papers for Edexcel, papers 2 and 3 for AQA and papers 1 and 3 for OCR consist of pre-issued case studies. The format of this paper is similar to that of the data-response paper but you are provided with a much more detailed and in-depth scenario. The questions test higher order skills i.e. they focus on assessing your ability to analyse and evaluate situations. The overall mark allocation for the case study paper is much higher than for the data-response papers. It is important that you can understand and respond to the command words in the questions such as 'discuss' or 'evaluate'. These are explained in more depth below.

Case study questions often expect you to offer solutions to business problems or analyse situations and propose business actions. Frequently, case studies are used to integrate the assessment of various topic areas. For example, the AQA paper 3 case study examines elements of external influences and objectives and strategy at the same time.

Command words

The key to understanding the type of questions and the depth of response needed is to look at the command word given and the mark allocation of the question. This will help you formulate the type of answer needed and the amount of time you should allocate for your response. Very common mistakes in exam technique are that students either fail to develop arguments sufficiently or they over-develop answers to questions that require simple responses and so they run out of time on the final questions.

Short answer questions

The first questions on the data-response or case study paper are usually quite straightforward. They may require you to give a formal definition of a business term with perhaps a valid example or description of how it may be applied by a business.

Short answer questions usually have these command words or phrases:
- 'Define', 'Explain the term/meaning of ...', 'What is meant by ...' or 'State/identify'.

Explanatory questions

These need slightly more development and require you to offer relevant subject knowledge and an explanation of how it might apply to the scenario given.

These questions are usually identified by the command words or phrases:
- 'Explain', 'Outline', 'Distinguish between …' or they may require calculations.

Analytical questions

These need to be answered in more depth. They often require advantages and/or disadvantages of business actions or situations to be discussed. You need to demonstrate knowledge, apply it to the scenario or situation given and then consider further implications, knock-on effects or cause-and-effect relationships. You need to explain in detail the process whereby cause brings about the end result. To answer these questions well use a continuous prose style of writing in well structured and developed paragraphs. Remember, in Business Studies there are two sides to every situation.

Analytical questions usually have these command words or phrases:
- 'Examine', 'Explain why', 'Analyse' or 'Consider'.

Evaluative questions

This type of question requires you to reach a judgement. This can be either weighing up the relative strengths (pros and cons) of your arguments in order to reach a conclusion, or discussing the likelihood of factors occurring in order to develop a judgement of which factors should be considered the most important. Again, you must put your answer in the context of the scenario presented.

Evaluative questions can usually be identified by the command words or phrases:
- 'Evaluate', 'Discuss', 'To what extent' or 'Recommend'.

Quality of language

All exam papers now carry marks for the candidates' quality of language. These are in addition to the marks allocated to each question. They are there to assess your ability to write in continuous prose, expressing ideas clearly and fluently, through well-linked sentences and paragraphs and using appropriate language and terminology.

You must therefore try to use a fluid, well-structured style in your answers to questions. If you do have any time left, it is wise to proof read and check your work.

Levels-of-response marking

All Business Studies papers are marked using levels-of-response marking. This uses a number of descriptors against which your work is assessed. The table shows an example of an AQA levels-of-response marking grid **for an evaluative question** worth 12 marks.

	Content 3 marks	Application 3 marks	Analysis 3 marks	Evaluation 3 marks
Level 2	**3 marks** Good understanding shown	**2–3 marks** Sound application of issues to the case study	**2–3 marks** Sound analysis of issues to the case study	**2–3 marks** Logical evaluation given in context
Level 1	**1–2 marks** Some understanding shown	**1 mark** Limited application of issues	**1 mark** Limited analysis of issues	**1 mark** Evaluation shown but unsupported
Level 0	**0 marks** No relevant content	**0 marks** No application of issues	**0 marks** No analysis offered	**0 marks** No evaluation shown

Edexcel and OCR both use levels-of-response marking as well but in a vertical table rather than grid format. For example, a 12 mark levels-of-response table may well appear as:

Level 4　Evaluation of the relative importance of the advantages and disadvantages given in context (9–12)

Level 3　Analysis demonstrated by consideration of the impact on or implications for the business (6–8)

Level 2　Understanding of concepts and/or theories demonstrated/applied in context (4–5)

Level 1　Appropriate concepts/issues identified or candidate shows some knowledge (1–3)

- To attain full marks for this sort of question you must demonstrate all the different skills shown – content/knowledge, application, analysis and evaluation – and move through the levels of each skill. For example, a student who just provides a bullet point list for their answer would only be showing 'limited understanding' and would thus receive one or two marks for content, i.e. a level 1 response only.

- A single paragraph of continuous prose that develops an argument relevant to the scenario might well show level 1 content (2 marks), limited or sound application (1 or 2 marks), limited or sound analysis (1 or 2 marks). Total marks: maximum 6.

- An answer that offers good analysis of several points in a number of separate paragraphs, drawing to a logical conclusion or reasoned judgement, would receive top of level two marks for each skill area and hence a maximum of 12 marks.

- Important note: For AQA you can reach the top of each level independently, e.g. it is possible to reach level 2 for application and analysis but include no evaluation in your answer, thus scoring:

Content 3 marks, Application 3 marks, Analysis 3 marks and Evaluation 0 marks. Total marks: 9.

The AQA, OCR and Edexcel specifications for AS Business Studies are split into three modules. The tables below show how this book covers the topics for these examinations:

The topics covered by your specification

Module	AQA	Chapter in this book
1	Marketing	1
1	Finance	2
2	People	3
2	Operations Management	4
3	External Influences	5
3	Objectives and Strategy	6

Module	OCR	Chapter(s) in this book
2	Business Decisions and	1 & 2 and
3	Business Behaviour	3 & 4
1	Businesses, their Objectives and Environment	5 & 6

Note: Business Decisions and Business Behaviour are integrated modules covering the four key topics covered in chapters 1–4.

Module	Edexcel	Chapter(s) in this book
2	Marketing and Production	1 & 4
3	Financial Management	2
1	Business structures, objectives and external influences	5 & 6

Note: Elements of Chapter 3 (People) are relevant for both module 1 and 2 for Edexcel.

Chapter 7 (How to Approach the Pre-issued Case Study) is relevant for all exam boards, although the example given is based on the June 2004 AQA examination.

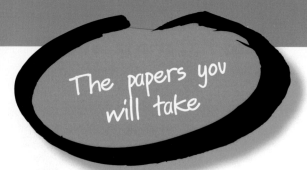
The papers you will take

AQA

For the AQA Business Studies exam, you have to sit three papers. Each paper examines two modules of study. For AQA these papers are:

- Marketing and Accounting and Finance — Two data-response questions of 1 hour. 30% of AS award
- People and Operations Management — Questions on the pre-released case study (1 hour). 30% of AS award
- External Influences and Objectives and Strategy — Questions on the pre-released case study (1 hour). 40% of AS award

You need to answer all the questions on each paper.

Note: Papers 2 and 3 (People, Operations Management, External Influences and Objectives and Strategy) are examined through one pre-released case study. To make revision easier, these are treated as separate topic areas in chapters 3, 4, 5 and 6. However, the final exemplar 'question to try' case study at the end of Chapter 6 is an integrated assessment combining External Influences and Objectives and Strategy as per the questions on a real Paper 3.

OCR

For the OCR Business Studies exam, you have to sit three papers. Each paper examines one module of study. For OCR these papers are:

- Businesses, their objectives and environment — Five compulsory questions based on a pre-released case study (1 hour). 30% of AS award
- Business decisions — Four compulsory questions based on data-response (45 minutes). 30% of AS award
- Business behaviour — Four compulsory questions based on a pre-issued case study (1 hour 15 minutes). 40% of AS award

You need to answer all the questions on each paper.

Edexcel

For Edexcel, all the exam papers are based on a common pre-released case study. For Edexcel the papers are:

- Business structures, objectives and external influences — Three compulsory questions (1 hour). 30% of AS award
- Marketing and Production — Three compulsory questions (1 hour). 40% of AS award
- Financial Management — Three compulsory questions (1 hour). 30% of AS award

Sample questions, model answers and questions to try are reflective of the types of questions on which you are examined. This book is split into discrete topic areas to aid revision and chapters are not intended to be exact models of examination papers.

Before the exam

- Plan your time – use a revision timetable.

- Make sure your notes are organised into topics and exams and that you have covered the entire specification.

- Practise past papers as much as possible. This will help your exam technique and subject knowledge.

- Analyse past papers for topics that have not been examined for a while. Use these as a focus point to start your revision.

- Revise your weakest areas of each topic first – then you've got plenty of time to cover them.

During the exam

- Read the paper carefully and absorb the material. Remember to use the items to help you. If you don't use them when the question tells you to, you will be throwing marks away. A good idea is to underline key points.

- Make a brief plan before writing. This helps you stay focused on the question and prevents you forgetting key points as you develop your response.

- Allocate time sensibly. Use the marks available and the command words as a guide as to how much to write and at what level.

- A simple point, but read the questions. If the question says advantages just do advantages and vice versa. If it says give two reasons, then give two. Make sure you're doing what the question asks, not what you think it asks.

- Use paragraphs to show the examiner when you are starting a new point or demonstrating a new skill.

- Always fully show your working for numerical questions. Then, even if you've got it wrong, you can receive some marks for method.

- Play the game. Understand what the examiners are looking for and provide it. Use proper terminology and avoid slang and jargon. Stay focused and don't use sweeping statements such as 'all business will...'. There are usually two sides to any business action and things 'may' or 'might' happen.

Focussing on the future, developing a clearer picture

In 1964 three engineers saw the rapid expansion of the camera market for domestic users and thought that there was room for another manufacturer. Thus, after talking to various banks and other prospective financiers, they formed Tajitsu Limited. Although based in a medium-sized factory just outside Leeds the company name was chosen to add flavour to the product (initially a self-focusing SLR camera) and make it stand it out in the market place. Over the following years it appeared that the initial idea was reaping great rewards as camera sales grew and grew, so that in 2001 sixty per cent of the over thirties age bracket in the UK owned a camera.

Priding themselves on being innovative and proactive, the original board of directors of Tajitsu invested heavily in research and development to keep up with competitors and to develop new products. They succeeded in keeping Tajitsu's respectable share of the UK market, helped primarily by being the first company to develop the unique selling point of automatically printing the date and time on the back of photographs when they were developed. Being aware of increasing competition from overseas, Tajitsu protected its share of the market by gradually catering to an increasing niche market that wanted more from their cameras than just the ability to point and shoot. This was again achieved by applying the concepts of innovation and forward thinking and Tajitsu developed a selection of specialist lenses and filters for their range of cameras.

However, over the past five years, with the advent of digital technology and desktop editing, Tajitsu has started to see its market share gradually fall (see table below) and sales start to decline, which is of particular concern in a market that is still growing. The original board of directors has gradually been replaced over the last four decades and the existing board faces a dilemma. Several suggestions as to how Tajitsu should progress with their immediate future have been put forward. First, has been the recommendation of the use of extension strategies to try to maintain Tajitsu's current position. Second, has been a proposal that Tajitsu needs to conduct extensive market research to try to determine future customer requirements and develop a more competitive position. Finally, a proposal has been put to the board for the possible take over by German rivals, KameraMeister. However, the board see this as a final solution as KameraMeister have outlined their intention to close UK manufacturing operations, stop the production of Tajitsu cameras altogether, and shift the production of specialist lenses, filters and equipment to their plant in Koblenz.

Tajitsu percentage market share	
2000	8.3%
2001	8.2%
2002	8.0%
2003	7.8%
2004	7.4%

(a) What is meant by the term 'unique selling point'? [2 marks]

(b) Outline **two** drawbacks a company like Tajitsu may face as a result of falling market share. [6 marks]

(c) **(i)** Explain the term 'extension strategy'. [2 marks]

   (ii) Analyse the usefulness of applying extension strategies to a company currently in Tajitsu's situation. [6 marks]

(d) Assess the extent to which conducting extensive market research might help a company gain a competitive edge over its rivals. [9 marks]

DAVID'S ANSWER

(a) What is meant by the term 'unique selling point'? [2 marks]

The term 'unique selling point' refers to the fact that the business has something different about it. For example, it has a unique location for selling its products that other businesses don't sell in.

0/2

How to score full marks

- David's answer in the first sentence is **far too vague, containing no use of business terminology**.

- **When defining business terms you need to be specific.** A unique selling point (USP) is something that **no other business possesses**. A USP can be perceived, that is created by advertising or **real**, for example a patented invention.

- **The second part of his answer tries to give an example of what he means.** This is a good technique as it makes it absolutely clear to the examiner what it is you are trying to express. In this case David's example is incorrect. A USP is a **feature of a product** that can be highlighted to differentiate it from competitors. Good examples could include POLO mints, Dyson vacuum cleaners or Nokia phones without aerials.

- The marks available for this question would be split into two levels: **level 1 for some understanding** and **level 2 for good understanding**. In this case David **shows no clear understanding at all** and so scores zero.

(b) Outline **two** drawbacks a company like Tajitsu may face as a result of falling market share. [6 marks]

Market share can either be measured in terms of a company's sales value or sales volume. From the data in the table it can be seen that Tajitsu's market share has fallen from 8.3% to 7.4%. This is an overall drop in share of 0.9% or 10.8% of their original market.

Two drawbacks that they may face because of this are that Tajitsu are losing customers and the fact that they have lost market share means that their advertising campaigns aren't very good and need to be adjusted to gain more customers. This means that Tajitsu will have to spend more on advertising and promotion than rival companies to keep their customers or attract new ones and this will increase the company's costs, especially in a competitive market where a lot of the basic products are the similar.

5/6

13

How to score full marks

- The mark scheme for a question like this would be: **Content 2, Application 4**. David scores marks as follows: **Content 2, Application 3**.

- Although David has scored a relatively high mark, he has made some **common mistakes when it comes to dealing with this type of question**.

- David's first paragraph is essentially correct – he has analysed the data and correctly calculated the fall in market share. **However, David is not actually answering the question that has been asked**. He will not lose any marks for doing this but, he has penalised himself by performing needless calculations and wasting time.

- In his second paragraph, David starts to address the issue, but has again fallen into a common trap. A falling market share does **not** necessarily mean that the company's sales are falling as well, especially in a market (such as the one given in the scenario) that is still growing. The company could actually be facing increasing sales but at a slower rate than their competitors, thus causing an overall decrease in market share.

- The second point David makes in this paragraph is expressed well and is fully relevant to the question. To make sure that he is achieving a good level of response for this argument, **David then relates his answer to the context of the question** by identifying the fact that this is a competitive market. This allows the examiner to move David into the top response level as he has expressed and developed a good point of knowledge and made it relevant to the company.

- David has, however, only developed one significant point. **To gain full marks he needed to explain another drawback in detail**. He could have included the fact that Tajitsu's range of pricing options will be limited as they must pay attention to the pricing strategies of the market leaders and follow suit or they may end up losing even more market share. Alternatively, Tajitsu may find it increasingly difficult to convince retailers to stock its products as rival brands become better known and thus demanded by consumers.

(c) (i) Explain the term 'extension strategy'. [2 marks]

Extension strategies mean that a company has a product that has entered the maturity stage of the product life cycle and that they are going to try to keep sales levels high and lengthen the product's life cycle before it enters the decline stage. An example could be developing new flavours for an existing product like POLO did.

2/2

How to score full marks

- The marks available for this question would again be split into two levels: **level 1 for some understanding** and **level 2 for good understanding**. In this case David **shows very clear understanding and so gains full marks**.

- This is an excellent answer. **David has remained focussed on the actual term and explained it using relevant business terminology**. Again he has included an example to reinforce his earlier description.

- This answer allows David to achieve the top of level two in levels-of-response marking. For a question requiring a **definition** or **explanation** of a term, there will be **two response levels in the mark scheme** relating to knowledge or content. A vague or poorly expressed answer would achieve a level one mark at best.

(c) (ii) Analyse the usefulness of applying extension strategies to a company currently in Tajitsu's situation.

[6 marks]

There are many different types of extension strategy that they could employ in their current situation. Firstly, they could increase the amount of money that they are spending on advertising and promotion and try to boost sales by using techniques such as money-off vouchers or free film development when you buy one of their cameras or they could try to get a famous celebrity or photographer to endorse their product. This means that if someone likes this celebrity they then may choose one of Tajitsu's cameras instead of a rival's.

Or they could try to attract customers by adding extra features to their cameras like the anti-red eye flashes for example. This should help attract more customers, as they will feel like they are getting more value for money. Overall extension strategies will help a company maintain its position and market share by convincing more customers to buy the product.

④/6

How to score full marks

- The mark scheme for an analytical question like this would be: **Content 2, Application 2, Analysis 2.** David's four marks were awarded as: **Content 2, Application 2, Analysis 0.**

- David has raised some valid points and written a fairly well-reasoned response. However, **he is answering what he thinks is the question rather than what the question actually asks.** David's response concentrates on extension strategies that the company could employ, rather than examining whether or not the use of such strategies would prove helpful to Tajitsu.

- This means that he is identifying and explaining relevant factors only, instead of **analysing the implication of employing such strategies.** In this instance, David achieved **a good mark for content** and/or relevant knowledge, **but has not achieved any marks for analysis.**

- In the first paragraph David again makes a **very common error.** Increased expenditure on advertising and promotion activities is not an extension strategy. Extension strategies are used to lengthen the product life cycle, as David described in part (c) (i), and are employed in the maturity or decline phase. Increasing advertising as a method of boosting or maintaining sales can be employed at any stage of the product life cycle, especially during launch or growth stages and so cannot be considered as an extension strategy in this context.

- David's second paragraph is more relevant. Here, he has described a strategy that involves redesign and development of the product; whether or not the product already has these features is irrelevant, David has used them as **good examples** of ways in which the company could extend its products and described the effects this might have on sales, as well as relating his answer to the context of the business, i.e. cameras.

- However, **he has still missed the key point of the question, which is to analyse their usefulness to a company in Tajitsu's position.** To get the full marks on this question, David would have had to identify the fact that extension strategies are only short-term solutions and that in a technologically fast-moving market their actual usefulness, as a tool to postpone the obsolescence of Tajitsu's products, will be limited. Arguments centring on the cost of redesigning or repositioning the product in the market, as against the limited benefit Tajitsu would receive, would be a good area to examine here.

(d) Assess the extent to which conducting extensive market research might help a company gain a competitive edge over its rivals. [9 marks]

Market research can be conducted in many different ways. Primary research is the collection of original data by the company itself whereas secondary research, sometimes called desk research, is when the company uses data collected by other companies or agencies to base its research on. The idea of market research is to find out what it is that customers actually want from a product so that businesses can then make it for them.

By conducting market research the company will find out more facts about the people that actually buy its product. Alternatively they may find out why some people don't buy their product and what it is that would actually make them want one. From this then the business can make a product that people will buy and target it to the people. The business should then start to make more sales and profits, improving their competitiveness in the market place. They will also be able to make their advertising much better as they can aim their advertising at the people in the right place at the right time. This means that they will not have to spend as much money to attract customers and again will help them become better in the market place.

On the other hand, market research can be very expensive and the cost of doing it needs to be less than the extra customers the business might gain as result. Alongside this, market research can be wrong or inaccurate since in primary research people may lie or there may be bias. If the company uses secondary research then the data may not be exactly what the company wants, leading them to make wrong decisions about what they should do. This could be very costly for a company if they go to all the time and trouble of developing a new product and then discover that no-one wants it. This will make their competitive position worse as they have spent a lot of money for no money in return.

However, it is my opinion that it is better to do some research than none at all as at least you then know a bit about what the customer wants.

7/9

How to score full marks

- The mark scheme for a question like this would be: **Content 2, Application 2, Analysis 3, Evaluation 2.** David scores his seven marks as follows: **Content 2, Application 2, Analysis 3, Evaluation 0.**

- Like so many students, David has not left enough time for the final part of this question and does not express himself fluently. However, this is a very good answer that is lacking in only one key area.

- **First, David has identified that the key word 'assess' in the question title means he has to consider the pros and cons of the argument.** This he has done quite effectively in paragraphs two and three. The first paragraph is really displaying basic textbook knowledge and is worthy of only a few marks as the question doesn't ask him to explain methods of market research.

However, low levels-of-response marks are available in the mark scheme for demonstration of knowledge as in this example.

- Paragraphs two and three do develop the point and David relates his line of argument to how market research can improve or decrease a company's competitive position, which is exactly what the question asks for. **This is a good example of an answer that considers both sides of the argument and remains tightly centred on the core of the question** and enables David to get **top level marks for analysis**.

- **David has also realised that 'assess' means 'evaluate' and that his answer will require some form of judgement at the end.** It is at this stage that he fails to score full marks for this question. David has reached a conclusion, but it is statement **not a reasoned argument**. In order to gain full marks here, you need to consider the circumstances in which market research is or is not needed. In the context of this question – a fast-moving technology based market – market research is essential if firms wish to gain or maintain a competitive edge as consumer wants and needs will be changing all the time. This though, is not true of all markets. How much market research would a company in a pure monopoly situation need to conduct?

- You also need to say that the company's need for market research would depend on what competitors are doing. If competitors are conducting market research and developing better and improved customer profiles and products, then unless the company does the same it might eventually lose any competitive edge that it once had.

Don't forget ...

You don't have to answer questions in the order that they are set. As long as you clearly identify on your script which question you are answering, play to your own strengths and first answer questions where you feel you have the best knowledge.

Make sure you leave enough time to answer the final question, as this will usually be worth the most marks. Having to rush your answer can lead to a less fluent writing style, as in David's answer to part (d). This makes it harder for the examiner to follow your arguments and award higher marks.

Although this question is about marketing, don't be afraid to draw on other areas. In part (d), for example, an argument based on how increased borrowing to finance extensive market research could affect the company's gearing ratio and financial stability would also have been entirely relevant.

Stay focussed on the question. Students often get wrapped up in their own arguments and actually forget what question they're meant to be answering. Re-read the question after each paragraph you write so you stay focussed.

Don't forget ...

A simple point, but often missed, **is to know the meaning of the key command words in the question and look at the mark allocation.** These tell you roughly at what level you need to answer the question and the depth you need to go into. (See pages 6 and 7 for an explanation of key command words).

When asked to define or explain a term, don't just copy out text from the scenario; this will gain you no marks. **Try to use different words and business terminology. Use an explanatory example where possible** – this will help you gain an extra mark if you are struggling to explain exactly what you mean.

To gain high marks on levels-of-response questions (see page 8) **try to develop one or two in-depth key arguments rather than a series of weak or superficial points.** Levels of response mean that as your arguments develop more depth and insight, you move into higher mark bands. If you don't attempt to expand on relevant points, you will not be able to move into the higher levels of response for each question.

For AQA candidates, the last question on each data response item will always require you to assess or evaluate. **This means you must weigh up the pros and cons of a situation and reach a reasoned judgement** – are any factors more relevant than others, is there any difference in timescale or what in your opinion is the most important issue?

If a question requires quantitative calculations or representations, make sure you present your answers clearly and logically, **showing full working, labels and annotations.** Even if you do not get the answer correct, there are stages of marks along the way so you may gain some, if not all, but only if the **examiner can see what you are doing.**

Marketing questions can often involve the interpretation of statistical information or calculations involving changes in pricing policies. **Make sure you have a calculator for any marketing exam.**

Key points to remember

Market analysis allows a business to better understand the needs of customers and to base its strategy on them, so it can anticipate consumer requirements rather than react to changed circumstances.

Market analysis may focus on **identifying**:
- the size of the market, changes and possible future trends
- sales volumes, values and market share
- market segments (different groups or types of consumer) and their varying needs and on **understanding**
- how consumers perceive a product's 'position' in a market, i.e. how it differs from its competitors.

The types of information used are:
- **quantitative** – data from a large group of respondents showing numbers, proportions or trends within a market, e.g. how many people buy a particular product
- **qualitative** – more detailed information from a smaller group of respondents about their views and opinions, e.g. why people buy a particular product.

This information can be gathered using:
- **primary** research methods – collecting new and original, first-hand information, e.g. by conducting a consumer survey
- **secondary** research methods – using existing, already published information, e.g. government statistics.

Sampling involves choosing a small group of people to be representative of a much larger population. It is used when doing primary research because it would cost too much and take too long to interview all potential customers.
- The sample must be large enough to produce reliable findings so that the results are typical of an average of the population.
- The method of sampling must be carefully chosen to avoid bias. Possible methods include **random sampling** (everyone has an equal chance of being questioned) and **quota sampling** (where the sample is made up of smaller groups of respondents, e.g. set proportions of males and females).

Market segmentation splits the market into groups of people which share distinct characteristics and makes each group separate from another. Examples of segmenting a market include:
- **Demographically** – according to the age/sex or cultural structure of the population.
- **Occupationally** – according to type of profession.
- **Behaviouristically** – according to the type of purchase or the way the product is used.
- **Geographically** – by country, region or post code area.
- **Socio-economically** – according to social class and income levels, i.e. class A, B, C1, C2, D and E.

Marketing objectives are the specific goals that a business is seeking to achieve through its marketing. These will depend upon the overall (corporate) aims of the business, as well as the constraints under which the business is operating, e.g. the availability of finance or the state of the economy.

Typical marketing objectives include:
- Increasing sales revenue and profitability
- Achieving growth of market share
- Successfully differentiating a product from its competitors
- Building customer satisfaction and loyalty
- Developing new products or new markets.

Key points to remember

A **marketing strategy** aims to achieve the current marketing objectives. It plans how best to 'add value' to a product, i.e. to create a willingness in the consumer to pay a price above that which it cost to make. This can be achieved through a **unique selling point** (USP) – a feature that differentiates a product from its competitors – or by achieving the right mix of design, function, image and service.

- **Niche marketing** aims a product at a specific, tiny market segment, focussing on **low volume sales** and **high profit margins**. Niche marketers can often avoid competition and focus on the needs of consumers. Over-reliance on a small market is risky – larger businesses may ultimately squeeze them out.

- **Mass marketing** targets a product at most or all of the market, aiming for high **volume of sales** with **low profit margins**. This strategy suits products with no obvious USP, but it can sometimes fail to meet the needs of individual consumers. Businesses may react by marketing different versions of a product to different groups of people, e.g. one model of a car marketed to families, another to business executives.

The **Boston Matrix** is a tool a business can use to assess what type of products it has and where it has gaps in its product portfolio. By categorising its products as 'Problem Children', 'Stars', 'Cash Cows' or 'Dogs', it can seek to achieve a balance that will ensure cashflow and profitability.

Companies also need to identify where their products are on the product life cycle. This helps them plan levels of expenditure on advertising, promotion strategies and research and development. However, each product's life cycle is different and so its usefulness as a forecasting tool is very limited.

Marketing tactics need to be planned carefully using these marketing tools:

- product
- price
- promotion
- place (or distribution).

Market analysis should ensure the **marketing mix** of these four features meets the needs of the target market. The marketing mix is also affected by factors such as the nature of the market, the degree of competition and the availability of finance.

The **product** is the most important aspect of the marketing mix, upon which the others depend. The product's use, design, appearance, life cycle and USP must be considered.

The **price** of a new product may be set by 'skimming' (setting a high price to reflect a product's initial uniqueness) or by '**penetration pricing**' (a low price to undercut established products). **Brand leaders** may be sold at a premium but **price takers** are simply priced in line with the competition. Prices may be based on costs of production, building in a profit margin (**cost-plus**) or a contribution towards fixed costs. Finally, a business should consider pricing tactics such as **loss leaders** (setting price below the cost of production) or **psychological pricing** (£9.99 instead of £10).

Promotion of the most appropriate message for the product can use:

- '**above the line**' methods using independent media such as TV or radio

- '**below the line**' methods which the firm itself controls, e.g. direct mail or trade fairs.

Distribution is crucial to ensure the product reaches the **right place at the right time**. The most appropriate **channel of distribution** could be retailers, wholesalers or direct selling.

Elasticity of demand for the product measures how much demand changes in proportion to a change in price or consumers' incomes. Demand is **elastic** if it changes more than proportionately to a change in price or income. It is **inelastic** if it changes very little in response to these factors. However, many businesses do not know their exact elasticity figures and even if they did, many would still use strategies such as competitive or cost-plus pricing.

A breath of fresh air

Transcendental Products came about following a trip to Thailand by Helen Myhill in 1994 during a year out from university. In the course of her travels she discovered that many of the products she and her student friends enjoyed were very much cheaper in areas of Asia than they were when purchased from retail outlets back home.

Having just completed her second year of a degree in business and marketing Helen was aware of some of the potential opportunities available as well as potential pitfalls presented by this situation. She spent the rest of her travels gathering information and contacts. Upon her return home, she convinced her parents to provide the initial financial backing for launching an import operation and acquiring a permanent market stall in their local town square.

Ten years later Helen's business has gone from strength to strength. Following a successful expansion programme of opening similar stalls in other regional towns, she recently negotiated a franchise deal with a nationwide chain of department stores that would allow her to set up a small Transcendental Products retail point in each of their stores.

However, as the popularity of such items has grown amongst differing market segments, Helen is now facing increasing competition from some European manufacturers who are flooding the market with cheap mass produced imitation goods like incense sticks, oil burners and natural oils. Estimated figures for the price elasticity of demand for incense sticks are given below.

Over recent weeks Helen has become increasingly concerned that opening the new franchise points may not be the correct direction for her company to take, especially as she seems to be losing a considerable amount of custom to more widely available cheaper alternatives. She is currently considering other forms of distribution channel that may be available to her. Helen has employed the services of a local business consultant who has advised her that to continue with her plan for the franchise outlets she needs to: concentrate on the more discerning customer at the luxury end of the market, diversify her product range to include more quality Asian products and differentiate herself from the mass market competition.

Question to try

Estimated figures for the price elasticity of demand for incense sticks (packet of ten)

Price in pence	Quantity demanded in thousands per year
70	100
68	104
66	108
64	112
62	116
60	120

Source: Researched by J. Harvey Business Consultancy Services Ltd.

(a) Explain the meaning of the terms 'diversify' and 'differentiate'. [4 marks]

(b) Outline two benefits to be gained from a business operating in a niche market. [4 marks]

(c) **(i)** Assume the price of incense sticks rises from 62p to 66p. Calculate the apparent price elasticity of demand. [2 marks]

 (ii) Analyse the benefits that a company might gain from operating in a market where demand is price elastic. [6 marks]

(d) Evaluate the factors that might influence the choice of distribution channel for a business in the current situation of Transcendental Products. [9 marks]

Examiner's hints
● For part (c) you do not have to be able to answer part (i) to answer part (ii).
● In part (d) note that the question says 'evaluate'. This means you must come to some conclusion about the relative weight and/or merit of your arguments or, alternatively, highlight factors that will have a definitive influence on the decision to be made.

Answers can be found on pages 94–96.

The Bluebird Inn, Tyll Goed

Tyll Goed is a small village in the picturesque area of the Vale of Glamorgan, approximately six or seven miles from Cardiff city centre. It is a popular destination for city dwellers at the weekend and also benefits from a small trade of tourists visiting the Welsh Folk Museum. Nick and Liz O'Sullivan own the 18th Century Bluebird Inn. With the aid of both sets of parents they formed a private limited company to purchase the inn when it came on the market three years ago. The premises are freehold (i.e. they are not tied to any particular brewery) and Nick and Liz felt incredibly fortunate when their bid of £275 000 (including stock in trade) was accepted. However, despite a good reputation as a well-run establishment with a friendly atmosphere and a beautiful location, the inn has not, so far, been as profitable as Nick and Liz had hoped.

Following the birth of their son, the lower than expected profits are now becoming of particular concern. The couple and their four other shareholders have discussed a number of ways of increasing the business turnover and, hopefully, profits. At the moment the inn consists of a public bar, a lounge bar and a large children's/games room that opens onto the beer garden. The main proposal is to convert this games room into a restaurant. This has two main advantages: first, they feel that locals and tourists would use the restaurant and second, it would increase the asset value of the business.

Liz has already conducted some initial research into likely costs:

Upgrade existing kitchen facilities	£8 000
Redecoration and furnishing of games room	£37 000
Marketing and launch costs	£5 000
Total	**£50 000**

Nick and Liz intend to use £10 000 of their own savings but need another source to generate the remaining £40 000 investment. Liz wonders whether it would be possible to use any internal sources of finance to provide at least some of the further funding they require.

Alongside the set-up costs researched by Liz, Nick has carried out some simple calculations as to the likely running costs and revenues from the proposed restaurant.

Average price per person per meal	£12
Variable cost per meal (labour and materials)	£4.50
Additional fixed cost per month from restaurant operations	£1125

Preliminary market research indicates that Nick and Liz would have an average of 250 customers per month, with the peak days being Friday and Saturday each week.

Following all this background research Liz is now very keen to put the proposal to the other investors and proceed with the project. However, Nick is still rather nervous – the other shareholders have already expressed an unwillingness to invest any further funds in the business and he is not sure of the accuracy of their market research.

(a) Explain the meaning of the term 'internal source of finance'. [2 marks]

(b) Outline **two** ways that it would be possible to raise the required finance. [6 marks]

(c) Calculate:

    (i) The break-even number of customers each month. [3 marks]

    (ii) The anticipated average monthly net profit, assuming the market research figures are accurate. [5 marks]

(d) Assess the usefulness of performing a break-even analysis to Nick and Liz in these circumstances. [9 marks]

SHERI'S ANSWER

(a) Explain the meaning of the term 'internal source of finance'. [2 marks]

An internal source of finance means that it comes from within the business not from outside, i.e. it is generated by the business itself not from another external source. Examples would include items like retained profits or money raised from selling assets.

2/2

How to score full marks

- This is a good concise answer showing clear understanding of the term. The first sentence starts as a rather general statement, but Sheri clarifies this and **makes a clear distinction** between internal and external sources and so would receive full marks.

- The marks available for definition type questions are always split into two levels: **level 1 for some understanding** and **level 2 for good understanding**. In this case Sheri **demonstrates that she understands the precise meaning of the term** and so would score two marks for achieving level 2.

- Sheri then **uses two correct examples** to demonstrate exactly what she means. This is a **very effective way to support your answer**. In this case the inclusion of the examples wasn't actually necessary to achieve full marks. However, sometimes these definitions carry a weight of three marks and this is a good way to make your answer more detailed and relevant and to ensure you score the third mark.

(b) Outline **two** ways that it would be possible to raise the required finance. [6 marks]

One possible way they could raise the money would be to approach a bank and ask for a loan. This would enable them to obtain the extra money they want for the restaurant. They would have to pay this money back but this could be done over a long period of time involving small monthly payments. However, they would have to pay back interest and the bank will also want some form of security before it gives them a loan, for example a cashflow forecast.

A second possible source would involve them selling some extra shares on the stock market. By this method they could raise a large sum of money without needing anyone's permission. However, there is a danger here that Nick and Liz could lose control of their business if they sell too many shares.

 3/6

How to score full marks

- This type of question requires **an explanatory answer that is in context to the business scenario given**. The mark scheme available would be: **Content 2, Application 4**. Top level marks for application would be given for responses which are directly related to the businesses circumstances. For her response, Sheri would score: **Content 1, Application 2**.

- This is a very disappointing answer to a fairly standard question.

- The first paragraph introduces one relevant source of finance, but the development of this point is limited. Sheri restricts her answer to textbook knowledge only; she **fails to relate her answer to the context and circumstances** of the question. For example, one of the business's problems is its low profit that may make it difficult to obtain a loan and high interest payments over a long-term loan could weaken profitability even more.

- Two marks on this question are available for content/knowledge and **four marks for application (relating theory to the given scenario)**. Sheri achieves low marks for application here as she is offered limited development only.

- The second potential source of finance that Sheri identifies is not appropriate (private limited companies do not sell shares on the stock market) and so does not receive any credit.

- To obtain the rest of the marks, Sheri would need to **develop another relevant source of finance** and relate it to the business's circumstances. One possibility would be to invite new investors to become shareholders (the discussion of dilution of ownership and control would then have become a viable statement). Alternatively, the company could take out a mortgage on the property they already hold. Sheri's answer nearly develops this point when she mentions the bank may require security. However, a cashflow forecast is not a method of securing a loan.

(c) Calculate:　　**(i)** The break-even number of customers each month.　　[3 marks]

Break even $= \dfrac{\text{Fixed costs}}{\text{Contribution (per unit)}}$

where contribution = Selling price per unit − Variable cost per unit.
$= £12 - £4.50$
$= £7.50$

Therefore break even $= \dfrac{£1125 \text{ per month}}{4.50}$
$= 150$

Thus 150 customers are required to break even each month.

How to score full marks

- Arithmetic questions are marked using **levels-of-response mark schemes**. A typical example like this would be: **Content 1, Application 2**.

- This is a very good answer. Although it contains an individual arithmetic notation error, it still receives full marks: **Content 1, Application 2**.

- Sheri has laid her work out clearly, starting with the relevant formula and continued to **develop her answer by labelling key figures**. This has helped Sheri as she made a mistake when she wrote down the calculation for break even. She has written the variable cost figure, not the contribution of £7.50. However, she has used the correct figure in her calculation and thus obtained the right answer. The examiner is able to see that although there is an error, Sheri does understand the appropriate concepts inherent in break-even analysis.

- It is always worthwhile making an attempt at this sort of question even if you are unsure as to the exact formula to apply. This sort of question is marked on levels of response and marks can be gained from an incorrect or inexact application of formula that **still demonstrates some knowledge** or understanding on the part of the candidate.

(c) Calculate: **(ii)** The anticipated average monthly net profit, assuming the market research figures are accurate. [5 marks]

Net profit   = Total revenue − Total costs

Total revenue = £12.00 × 250
              = £3000

Total costs   = Fixed cost + Variable costs
              = £1125 + (£4.50 × 250)
              = £1125 + £1125
              = £2250

Therefore,
net profit   = £3000 − £2250
            = £750

Assuming the market research is ok the restaurant should make £750 per month.

 5/5

How to score full marks

- Similar to part b (i), the marks available are for content and application but in this case are given as: **Content 2, Application 3**.

- This is a perfect answer by Sheri. As with the previous question she has started by **laying out the relevant formula** and proceeded to complete the question clearly showing all her workings, thus achieving full marks for content.

- Her actual workings are entirely correct, demonstrating that she applies her knowledge and she has thus received full marks. In this instance, she has shown a good understanding of the relevant theory as well as how to apply it, so **Content 2, Application 3** is given.

(d) Assess the usefulness of performing a break-even analysis to Nick and Liz in these circumstances.

[9 marks]

Break-even analysis has a lot of uses and as such its actual usefulness to different companies and people in different situations can be quite varied. Its use to Liz and Nick I will discuss below.

They could use it to help them decide whether or not they need a loan and how to plan the payments. It could also help them to decide if they might need an overdraft if the figures shown are lower than expected and future problems do occur.

Performing a break-even analysis could help them to produce a cashflow forecast – this they can then present to the bank manager to help them as security for obtaining a loan and to prove to the manager that they have planned ahead.

The market research they have done may be inaccurate or wrong and this could give a false impression of the business's financial position. The usefulness of break even depends on the accuracy of the information used. It could help future plans for refurbishment and the obtaining of a loan to pay for such development within the business. This would be very useful.

One problem with break-even analysis is that it assumes that Nick and Liz will sell all the meals that they produce in their restaurant and that they use all their ingredients at the same time. This is really not very likely to happen. If there is poor weather, especially on the weekend, then they are not going to get as many customers as they expected. Similarly people may decide to go on cheap summer holidays instead and this could lead to the results of their analysis actually been wrong.

Another good reason for them to use break-even analysis is that it is fairly easy to do. Nick and Liz may not know many other ways to forecast so they can use breakeven as it easy. This is quite good for small businesses.

6/9

How to score full marks

- This question as highlighted by the command word 'assess', requires you to demonstrate all the different skill areas. The mark scheme for this type of question would be: Content 2, Application 2, Analysis 3, Evaluation 2.

- Sheri's response here is of a mixed quality. She has made some good points on which she has based her answer and has applied her comments to the case, but has failed to develop them to a sufficient depth. She has offered a number of possible benefits for the use of break-even analysis and, recognising that this question requires a two-sided response, has also presented a brief commentary on the shortcomings of this technique. Finally, she has also attempted to relate it to the context of the scenario given and makes a weighted judgement on the overall position in the final paragraph of her response. For the answer above Sheri would have been given: Content 2, Application 2, Analysis 1, Evaluation 1. Total 6.

- **Her answer contains several flaws** that limit the level of marks she can receive. The first paragraph contains no information of any merit at all. Many students start questions like this as a way of introducing their response to a question but you should be aware that **an introductory paragraph that contains no actual factual information will receive few if any marks**.

- In the following two paragraphs, Sheri starts to offer information on why break-even could be useful, and loosely relates it to the circumstances of the business. However, **her points are not developed far enough to receive marks for analysis**. Each point is only briefly covered with a short explanation of its possible use. She should have **analysed the advantages and disadvantages** of break-even as an aid to decision-making. Again, she makes the mistake (as in her earlier answer) that this could then be used for security, which is not the case.

- In paragraph four, Sheri could have obtained high marks but, again, she has **failed to develop a relevant point sufficiently**. Accuracy of information is always an important aspect of any modelling or forecasting technique. However, Sheri fails to explore the implications or knock-on effects that using inaccurate information could actually have on the business. For example, inaccurate market research could have caused Nick and Liz to drastically overstock, which could be a major problem as their stock items include perishable goods. In her next statement though, Sheri does offer some development to her argument by stating some of the limitations of the basic assumptions in break-even analysis and the knock-on effect that this may have on the number of customers. However, the arguments she uses to present this idea are fairly weak, so she does not gain many marks.

- Finally, Sheri offers up a simple judgement about the usefulness of the analysis in the context of the question. This is a good idea as this **question does require evaluation as indicated by the command word 'assess'**. However, once again this is fairly limited. **Sheri fails throughout this question to discuss in depth the advantages and disadvantages of break-even** (such as being a static model in dynamic markets) and **does not reach a fully reasoned judgement about circumstances when break-even would be useful** ('what if' situations, for example).

- Sheri would have gained marks had she stated that break-even analysis (like any modelling or forecasting technique) is a **useful tool to help a business make decisions but it should not be the only information on which decisions are based**.

Don't forget ...

Try to match the time you spend on a question to the marks available for it. For AQA exams, each data-response question is worth 25 marks in total and there are two questions per paper in a 1 hour exam. Allowing for reading time, this means **you are aiming to gain approximately a mark per minute.**

Make sure that **you clearly label key figures as you work through a calculation.** If you make an error in your calculations and carry this error through, the examiner still needs to see you demonstrating knowledge and application. If you label figures and show all working it is possible to gain high marks, but only if the examiner can follow your processes.

An accounting and finance **paper will almost certainly require you to perform calculations.** Make sure you have the proper equipment and practise answering this type of question using past papers and case studies to build up your confidence.
The only real way to revise practical applications is to practise them.

The information in the case study **is there to help you.** Not all of it will be relevant to the questions asked. However, you need to be able to make basic assumptions about the type of business, market conditions, possible income and sources of finance for any business presented to you.

Make sure that **you know what level of exam skills a question calls for.** Some simple questions require only subject knowledge; others call for analysis or evaluation. The mark allocation and command word in the question provide guidance on this. Terminology is summarised in the section on exam skills in the Introduction (pages 6–7).

Don't be afraid to draw on other subject **areas.** Although a question may relate primarily to finance and accounts, drawing on subject matter from other topic areas can greatly enhance an answer. Remember **any financial decision taken is going to have a knock-on effect on production, personnel or marketing** considerations as well. The key is to keep your answer relevant and focussed on the question.

Never leave a question unanswered. Even if you are unsure of the exact formula to apply or the most relevant line of argument to use, **any information of merit contained within your response will be awarded marks.** However, if you do not attempt a question you will receive zero.

Costs, revenue and profit

Profit = Total revenue – Total cost

Total revenue = Selling price × Number
per unit   sold

Total cost = Fixed + (Variable cost × Number)
costs   (per unit   produced)

- **Fixed costs** do not change when output changes, e.g. rent and rates. They are usually examples of **indirect costs**, i.e. costs that do not relate directly to a particular product but are the general costs (**overheads**) of running the business.

- **Variable costs** change in direct proportion to the output of a firm, e,g. raw materials. They are usually also **direct costs**, i.e. a direct result of producing a particular product.

- Remember that **basic assumptions can be questioned**, e.g. fixed costs might not remain constant if capacity needs expanding.

Cash flow management

- Profit plays a vital role in the long-run success of a business, but in the short-term **cashflow** is the most essential factor in a business's survival.

- A business needs a sufficient supply of cash in order to conduct day-to-day operations. Without the ability to pay wages and suppliers on time an organisation may ultimately face liquidation.

- Cashflow forecasting and management concentrate on identifying, and avoiding, potential shortages of cash. Methods of improving cashflow include **factoring, sale and leaseback** and **working capital control**.

- You must be able to analyse how these solutions might impact on the rest of the business, e.g. a decision to remove trade credit to customers may encourage them to pay quicker, but may also encourage some customers to purchase elsewhere.

Break-even analysis

- **Break-even analysis** shows a business the minimum output it needs to produce and sell if total revenue is to cover total costs, i.e. at the break-even point, no loss or profit is being made.

- It can be extended to identify the **margin of safety** (the number of units that current output exceeds the break-even point) or expected levels of profit at differing levels of output.

- The **break-even point** can be shown on a diagram where the total revenue line cuts the total cost line.

  Break-even can also be calculated as:

  $$\frac{\text{Fixed cost}}{\text{Contribution per unit}},$$

  where

  Contribution = Selling price – Variable cost
  per unit   per unit   per unit

- Break-even analysis illustrates the impact that changes in costs, selling price or output levels will have on the business's profit or loss. However, it is an overly simplistic model of reality and so can be misleading, e.g. selling price and variable cost per unit are rarely constant over the whole range of output as simple break-even models assume.

Sources of finance

Virtually any decision a business makes is going to require financing in one way or another. Available sources include:

- Internal sources: retained profits, existing working capital and the sale of assets
- External sources: share capital, loans, overdrafts, debentures, venture capital or government grants.

The key is to identify the most appropriate source of finance depending on:

- the cost of the finance – in terms of interest re-payments or dividends
- the timescale – if an investment will bring benefits over a long period, a longer-term source of finance, such as a mortgage or share capital, will be appropriate
- the size and legal status of the business – limited companies have a wider range of options, including share capital
- the current gearing – the proportion of existing funds that have been obtained through borrowing.

Cost and profit centres

- Cost centres are areas in an organisation that are held accountable for their own identifiable expenditure. A profit centre is also accountable for its own revenue and so a separate profit and loss account can be drawn up.
- When areas of an organisation operate as independent cost or profit centres, staff in those areas can be very motivated as they have a degree of responsibility and trust, and are able to see and measure their own performance.

Budgeting

- Budgets are agreed financial plans of what a business expects to achieve, in terms of its targets for sales revenue and its limits for expenditure.
- Budgets provide an important means for managers to control expenditure in a business, highlighting waste or inefficiency. They also help improve coordination whilst allowing delegation. They provide managers with a valuable way of reviewing performance and planning ahead.
- The setting of budgets can be problematic. Forecasting of data could prove inaccurate and mistakes in one budget can have knock-on effects on others. The process of gathering data is itself time-consuming and can be difficult to coordinate. The process of budgeting can generate conflict and resentment amongst personnel as it will mean some projects or departments being prioritised over others.
- Budgets can also be delegated or devolved and in this way can prove to be motivating to employees or department teams who are given more responsibility and control.
- When comparing actual performance with budgeted figures, managers will be looking to explain any variances (differences) between the two.
- A favourable variance means the actual figure is better than the budget figure.
- An adverse variance means the actual figure is worse than the budget figure.

It is important to investigate the reason for any variance so that future budgets achieve zero variances.

Adverse conditions at Fletchers

Fletchers Fabrications make and supply single panel fabrications for assembly into varying sized storage facilities. Customers can tailor-make storage units for stocks of finished goods or materials by purchasing the number of panels needed for the size of unit they want and then either assemble it themselves or, for an additional fee, Fletchers will despatch an erection team to the customer's premises and assemble it for them.

Each panel requires a standard blend of raw materials, which are processed using an injection moulding technique and finished by skilled workers to an exacting standard. It is vitally important that every panel produced meets the specifications since failure to do so will result in finished units rapidly losing their integrity against the elements or, in a worse case, panels that will not fit together and so have to be scrapped. Fletchers employ various quality control methods to maintain their high standards, but also try to keep workers highly motivated to take a personal pride in the quality of their work. To this end each production employee works on a batch of panels from start to finish so that they are able to take satisfaction from starting and completing a total job.

Fletchers also employ a standard cost system and cost centres for the budgetary control of direct materials and direct labour. This helps them to maintain an effective system of budgetary control and price and quote on jobs effectively.

The following information relates to the last month's production.

Cost category	Budgeted	Actual
Production labour		
Direct hours	565	592
Rate of pay (per hour)	£8.00	£8.40
Production materials		
Usage (kg)	470	482
Cost (per kg)	£3.00	£2.60
Overheads	£30 000	£32 000
Sales revenue	£50 000	£50 000

During the month Fletchers completed all production targets and so the budgeted sales revenue figure and actual sales value invoiced are the same.

(a) Explain the meaning of the terms:

   (i) Standard cost system   [2 marks]

   (ii) Cost centre   [2 marks]

(b) Calculate the following variances for the month shown:

   (i) Direct labour variance   [3 marks]

   (ii) Direct materials variance   [3 marks]

   (iii) Profit variance   [5 marks]

(c) Evaluate the possible factors that may have contributed to the variances that have occurred.   [10 marks]

Examiner's hints
- For part (c) you are required you to **look at both sides of the argument and evaluate it in terms of a small business context.** This implies that your conclusion must revolve around the possible reasons for these variances occurring alongside reasoned judgements regarding what are the most likely factors.
- For part (b) **show all your working** for parts (i) and (ii). This will help when calculating part (iii). Be certain to clearly identify whether the variances are adverse or favourable.

Answers can be found on pages 97–99.

SYPI changing structure and performance

Situated on three main production sites and with two administrative centres, South Yorkshire Precision Instrumentation is one of the UK's leading manufacturers of high tech instrumentation. Their main activities are based around batch orders for the aeronautical and marine industries, but they also undertake the design and manufacture of specialist equipment for scientific and research purposes. They have a particular reputation for manufacturing instruments that are required to operate in highly stressful conditions and yet maintain pinpoint accuracy. In doing this the company has acquired an enviable client list including NASA and the US Geological Survey.

However, over recent months the board has been discussing the proposed future structure of the firm. They see this as a response to several factors including:

• Increasing European competition from manufacturers (mainly German and Swiss)

• Increasing global competition (especially from some Pacific Rim-based competitors)

The Board have identified that their industry is also currently undergoing a swift rate of change with new technologies been introduced and competitors undertaking new business strategies and structures. They have decided that they need to respond to these changes by introducing a new structure themselves. At the top of the list at the moment is a proposal to move toward a matrix management structure and to implement a drive toward a more modern, integrated and flexible corporate culture.

The Board believe these moves together with major investment in state-of-the-art technology should help maintain and improve SYPIs global competitive position (recently they have tendered for, but not won, a couple of lucrative contracts) and also improve the efficiency of its workforce.

The Board of SYPI have been in communication with the two major unions, that represent its blue- and white-collar workers respectively, throughout their deliberations and have welcomed the unions comments and ideas. One of the major points raised by the unions on their representatives' behalf is that employee satisfaction is the key to improving and maintaining the business's competitive performance.

However, the management believe that some of the issues regarding employee satisfaction should be assuaged by their proposal that a more efficient and productive workforce should mean higher profits and greater opportunities for future pay rises. In fact the Board have discussed the idea with the unions that an interim pay award of 2.5% for everyone should help ease the transitional period between the current and new structures and culture.

(a) What is meant by:

    (i) Corporate culture [3 marks]

    (ii) Matrix management structure? [3 marks]

(b) Explain ways in which a business such as SYPI could measure the efficiency of its workforce. [6 marks]

(c) Analyse the difficulties an organisation may experience when trying to restructure. [8 marks]

(d) Evaluate the importance of employee satisfaction to the relative competitive position of an organisation. [15 marks]

AMAR'S ANSWER

(a) What is meant by:

(i) Corporate culture? [3 marks]

Corporate culture involves the way in which a business operates. It is the whole personality of the business and determines the way in which everyone in that organisation acts.

2/3

(ii) Matrix management structure? [3 marks]

Matrix management involves the organisation of a business into non-linear departmental structures. It involves the creation of a two-sided structure in which employees belong to their functional area or department and also to a project or team. This means that each project or team should have all the expertise it needs on hand at any given time.

3/3

How to score full marks

- Short answer definition questions are divided into two levels: **level 1 for some knowledge of the term** and **level 2 for good knowledge**. For three mark definitions, it is always a reliable tactic to **include a supporting example** as well.

- **(a) (i)** Amar's answer in the first sentence is **fairly vague, though sufficient to show he has an idea**. The second part of his definition shows a little more understanding and depth. In order to score full marks you would need to state that corporate culture 'is the accepted code that affects the working practices, decision-making and management style of the business'. So for this answer Amar only receives **2 marks** or top of level 1.

- **(a)(ii)** **When defining business terms you need to be specific** as Amar is in his second definition. He has obviously learned this definition and is able to use good terminology in his explanation.

- Instead of giving a relevant example, Amar has used **the idea of stating an advantage of the system**. This is also a good exam technique to help demonstrate to the examiner the depth of your understanding, as relevant examples may be difficult to think of under exam pressures.

(b) Explain ways in which a business such as SYPI could measure the efficiency of its workforce.

[6 marks]

There are several ways in which a business like SYPI could measure the efficiency of its workforce. For the workforce as a whole the Board could look at figures such as the labour turnover or absenteeism rates. These measure how often employees leave the organisation or take sick days and are calculated using mathematical formula such as:

$$\frac{\text{Number of staff who leave per year}}{\text{Number of staff in total}} \times 100$$

or

$$\frac{\text{Number of staff absent}}{\text{Number of staff in total}} \times 100$$

If employees are leaving regularly or taking a lot of sick leave the efficiency of the organisation will fall. The organisation will either have to lose the production of that employee entirely or use someone who, to begin with, would be less efficient as they learn how to do the job. From these formulas, the higher the result, the worse the situation is.

SYPI is also a manufacturing organisation so the efficiency of manufacturing employees could be measured by looking at levels of output compared to number of employees. This can be done over a period of time to see if output per employee is falling or rising and so the management can see if efficiency is improving or not.

6/6

How to score full marks

- For a question such as this that asks you to **'explain'**, the examiners are looking for you to **demonstrate both knowledge and development**. Hence the mark scheme for this question would appear as: **Content 3, Application 3**. The top level of each skill would be awarded for **a good answer that was in context**.

- From this answer it is obvious that Amar is **strong on both subject knowledge and exam technique**.

- Amar has recognised that the command word for this **question 'explain' means he has to state the relevant factor or theory and then discuss briefly how it works or is applicable** to the situation given.

- Amar has fully addressed the question by giving **three possible ways** in which efficiency could be measured (this is sufficient for level one content/knowledge marks] and then briefly explained how each method can be used to determine whether efficiency is improving or not. This is exactly the type of approach to use for this type of question, as the question asks **'explain how'**, **not 'why'**. The inclusion of the actual formula was not entirely necessary given the strength of the rest of the answer. However, this is a good way of showing the examiner the level of knowledge you possess.

- A common error that students make on this type of question is to go into too much depth and start analysing the reasons for measuring efficiency or the benefits and drawbacks of different methods. In this instance, the only criticism of Amar's answer is that he has perhaps included a little too much information. **However, generally it is better to give too much than too little.**

- In the final part of his answer, Amar has **put the response in context and linked his answer to the SYPI's type of organisation**. (Doing this ensures you achieve marks for **application** on a levels-of-response mark scheme.) In this instance, Amar demonstrates clearly the relevant skills and so receives: **Content 3, Application 3**. Full Marks.

- You could have used examples of benchmarking, targets or budgetary controls or even the measurement of waste as compared to output. Any of these would have provided a relevant point to develop as long as you explained how they related to measuring efficiency.

(c) Analyse the difficulties an organisation may experience when trying to restructure. [8 marks]

Restructuring and changing working practices is a huge undertaking for many businesses and it is something that needs careful consideration as there are many things that can go wrong. When an organisation decides to restructure there are a lot of problems that they may face. Employees of the business may cause difficulties as they don't like the proposed ideas despite the offer of a pay award and it may prove difficult to get them to accept the change. This may be because as they don't want to accept the change and so may offer resistance to the management and board.

A second difficulty is that of costs. There will be an increase in the level of costs faced by the business and could be for several reasons. First, employees might make mistakes if they have been given a new job to do, or they might not know who to ask for information now. This makes the company less efficient and so costs rise. If the restructuring is major, as seems to be the case, then the business may face rising costs as production is slowed down or bought to a standstill while changes are made. Alternatively, new working methods may involve training the workforce in how to use them. All these factors take time and cost money and this could cause the business big problems in terms of losing profits, or being late on deliveries and may even affect their cash flow.

Thus there are lots of difficulties that could be experienced but the major ones are that employees may not like the idea and costs will probably rise while the changes take place.

How to score full marks

- An example of an eight mark scheme would be: **Content 2, Application 2, Analysis 4**. Note the marks are weighted towards demonstrating analytical skills. For Amar's answer above, he actually gained: **Content 2, Application 2, Analysis 3**.

- This answer is of varying quality. Amar's first paragraph **highlights a relevant factor and explains why it could be a problem but it does not contain any analysis**. His introductory sentences contain no information of any relevance or development at all. He then introduces a relevant factor but fails to explain the cause/effects or implications and why this would constitute a problem to the business. At this stage, therefore, he is limiting the marks he will get for his response as he has failed to develop it sufficiently.

- In the second paragraph, Amar has done exactly what is required to achieve high marks. Relevant factors have been selected and explained, thus demonstrating knowledge and development, and they have been analysed as well. **Amar has identified and developed the possible knock-on effects** these factors may cause and he has detailed why they might constitute a problem to the organisation. Amar achieves the higher-grade bands for levels-of-response marking, but because of the lack of development in the first paragraph, he does not achieve full marks.

- The final summary paragraph does not add anything new to the arguments already offered and so does not achieve any additional marks. **Make sure that every sentence of your response adds something new** or further development to your answer, otherwise you are just penalising yourself by wasting time.

(d) Evaluate the importance of employee satisfaction to the relative competitive position of an organisation. [15 marks]

Many things determine the competitive position of an organisation, not just whether or not the employees are satisfied. Factors such as the size of the organisation and what competitors are doing will have an influence on how well the organisation performs as will the state of the economy, if the business imports or exports and the level of exchange rates. Even the level of inflation will in some ways determine how well the business performs.

It also depends on the type of business or market the organisation is operating in. For example, employee satisfaction is more likely to be important in an organisation that is democratic or has an empowered culture. Similarly, autocratic managers are less likely to be worried whether or not employees are happy. Finally, it depends on the objectives of the business. If the business is managing to achieve its objectives it really doesn't matter whether or not the employees are satisfied as the business is achieving what it wants to achieve anyway. (8/15)

How to score full marks

- Typically the marks for a 15 mark evaluative question break down as: **Content 3, Application 3, Analysis 4, Evaluation 5**. Again the marks are weighted towards the higher order skills.

- Amar's answer reflects **a common error often made by AS candidates**. He demonstrates his understanding of exam technique by showing that he knows that the command word 'evaluate' means 'express a judgement'. The problem is that **Amar has done nothing *but* evaluate**, i.e. his answer consists entirely of evaluative factors. There is no discussion of relative pros and cons or influencing factors with a weighted judgement at the end that develops out of the arguments used. Amar's answer is pure judgement.

- In levels-of-response marking schemes, **marks are awarded for moving through the levels of different categories that demonstrate a variety of skills** (see page 8). In the first paragraph, Amar has merely presented a list of items with no development of these points. This means Amar can only be awarded level one for content/knowledge.

- In the second paragraph there is some development of factors and a definite judgement made, relating to these factors. This demonstrates evaluation. However, the **judgement made relies on assertion**. It is **not a logical conclusion stemming from a reasoned argument**.

- To summarise, the reason why Amar does not score full marks for the question is that he has failed to provide any analysis, i.e. there is no discussion as to how, why or whether employee satisfaction affects the competitive position of an organisation nor is it related to SYPI at all. Thus Amar will only receive: **Content 3, Application 1, Analysis 2, Evaluation 2**. Total 8.

- These are relevant lines of argument that could have been included:

  ○ Employees who possess a high degree of job satisfaction are more likely to be highly motivated than de-motivated. Highly motivated employees take less time off and are also less likely to leave a job they find satisfying, thus productivity should increase. The resulting reduction in costs from fewer staff absences or lower replacement costs alongside increased output should help improve the organisation's competitiveness.

  ○ Satisfied and happy employees are far less likely to become involved in industrial disputes with management. This also implies good communications between different levels of the hierarchy. Again a general cost saving and efficiency gain may be experienced here in comparison with competitors who might not have such good industrial relations.

  ○ However, achieving a more highly satisfied workforce could involve improving working conditions or training which may cost the organisation time and money. Does the benefit to be derived outweigh the cost of achieving it?

  ○ Some measures to improve competitiveness may result in unsatisfied and de-motivated workers, for example streamlining, de-layering or rationalisation of the organisation's activities.

- **In order to achieve full marks on a levels-of-response mark scheme you need to demonstrate the full range of skills that are being examined.**

Don't forget ...

When asked to 'identify', 'explain' or 'briefly describe' make sure that you not only state relevant points but that you **develop them by using relevant terminology and by giving an example** so that you pick up the full marks available for the question.

For questions that ask you to 'evaluate' or 'analyse', make sure you say something about **all major parts** of the question. Discuss advantages and disadvantages, pros and cons as well as writing a final statement containing your judgement.

In a question that asks you to 'evaluate' there are usually **several definitive factors**. State what they are and explain their relevance to the context of the business or scenario given.

Know the meaning of the key command words in the question and look at the mark allocation. These will tell you roughly at what level you need to answer the question and how much depth you need to go into. (See pages 6 and 7 for an explanation of key command words.)

When asked to give a specified number of reasons in a question, make sure that is **the minimum number of reasons that you give.** Also make sure that your reasons are genuinely different from each other – don't give the same reason twice just using different words.

Don't fall into the trap of being over-assertive and stating that this '**will**' happen or employees '**always**' do certain things. This is not the case. Businesses or employees often react in quite unexpected ways to circumstances, so you should always express that something '**may**' or '**might**' have a particular effect.

Use the case study or data-response item whenever possible, particularly when the information contains graphs, charts or statistics. They are there for a reason and candidates often make the mistake of ignoring this information when answering the questions. If you don't do this, it makes it difficult for you to pick up marks for **application** and for putting your answers **in context**.

When you are revising a particular theory, such as Maslow's or Herztberg's, make sure you learn a couple of advantages as well as a **couple of major criticisms**. Very few things in business studies are absolutes and **you need to be able to express both sides of an argument**.

Management structure and organisation

● The effective management of its employees is often the biggest challenge faced by an organisation, whatever its size.

● Managing change successfully depends on a flexible and open business culture (the way things are done). If relationships between managers and workers are strong, and two-way communication is the norm, then adapting to change will be easier.

● An efficient organisational structure provides a framework for the effective management of people. Hierarchies develop in a business to ensure clear accountability and responsibility. By adding layers of management, each manager's span of control (the number of subordinates responsible to them) is kept small and manageable. However, as hierarchies develop, chains of command lengthen and communication from top to bottom becomes more difficult.

● Some workers (perceived by managers as being Theory X) need close supervision whilst others (perceived by managers as being Theory Y) are motivated by the greater freedom and opportunity that a 'flatter' structure brings. No one type of structure is perfect for every business.

● There needs to be a balance between centralised decision making and delegation (passing down) of authority. Whilst centralisation brings control, coordination and expertise, decentralisation can offer the business flexibility and job satisfaction to subordinates.

● To avoid the problems of functional hierarchies based on a department structure, some businesses have turned to matrix management. This seeks to give individuals with specialist skills their own responsibilities within project teams. This creates flexibility and motivation but brings problems of coordination.

● Management By Objectives (MBO) provides an effective way of coordinating the activities of a business and improving decision making. MBO defines targets for an individual and then assesses the performance against these targets. A system of consultation is needed to produce mutually agreed targets and so works best where managers are willing to adopt a more democratic style. Rapid changes in business can make objectives out of date so the process can become time-consuming and bureaucratic.

Human resource management

● Effective workforce planning involves assessing changes in the number, type and skills of workers required in the future. It needs to take account of changes in the labour market; demographic changes (ageing population), social changes (more women 'returners') and legal, technological and political factors all influence the availability, willingness and cost of employees. Planning is important so that the business is able to recruit employees with the right skills.

● Workers can be recruited internally, e.g. through promotion, or externally by advertising for workers, using job centres, recruitment agencies or other methods. The choice of selection methods, whether it be interviewing or testing, must be appropriate to the job in question. Methods of recruitment and selection need to ensure the right person is chosen in a cost-effective way.

● Induction training is vital to ensure that a new employee is able to start working effectively. Subsequent training is designed to develop skills, to increase employee flexibility and to motivate through opportunities for self-development. These benefits must be weighed against the costs of training and the risk of trained employees being 'poached' by other firms. Methods of training can be on-the-job (whilst the employee is still working) or off-the-job (training away from the normal workplace). The choice of method will depend upon the circumstances and decision on cost-effectiveness.

Motivation

- A motivated workforce is interested and keen and is the key to business success. Motivation can help to reduce labour turnover and absenteeism, whilst boosting productivity and quality. Individual workers have different needs so businesses may experience motivation problems for different reasons. Solutions need to fit the circumstances, the time period and the types of individuals involved.

- Writers have disagreed over which factors are most important in motivating workers:

  - **Taylor** emphasised the **role of money** (through piece rates) in encouraging hard work and increased productivity.

  - **Mayo** focusses on the management's approach to **human relations**, consulting its workers and encouraging teamwork.

  - **Maslow's Hierarchy of Needs** suggests individuals initially seek financial security and then look to 'higher level' needs of self-esteem and achieving their full potential.

  - **Herzberg** argues that workers first need 'hygiene' factors to be met – to ensure the working environment is not a **dissatisfier** – and then they seek **motivators** such as increased responsibility and personal achievement.

- Financial incentives can include:

  - **Piecework** – paying an amount per unit produced

  - **Performance-related pay** – linking pay to the achievement of individual targets

  - **Profit sharing** – giving workers a share of the business's profits

  - **Share ownership** – rewarding workers with shares in the business

  - **Fringe benefits** – other perks such as company cars or pension schemes

  - **Salaries** – paying a stated annual sum for the carrying out of a role.

- Non-financial motivators include:

  - **Job enrichment** – extending the authority and responsibilities of a worker

  - **Job enlargement** – giving a worker more work of a similar nature

  - **Empowerment** – giving employees the authority to make decisions about their own activities

  - **Team working** – working in small groups towards a common target.

- Management styles include:

  - **Authoritarian** – the leader makes all the decisions alone

  - **Paternalistic** – the leader may consult and then makes decisions in the best interests of the workforce

  - **Democratic** – the leader allows workers to help make decisions.

The management style needs to be matched to the task in hand and the nature of the workforce. Authoritarian styles suit 'Perceived Theory X' workers and crisis situations, whilst democratic styles suit more experienced, 'Perceived Theory Y' workers. It is not always easy for managers to change their style, though, as their style reflects their personality. The need for a different style is often a need for a different manager.

Trouble at the top

Five years ago Fairchild Motors appointed a new Managing Director, Russell Freemantle. It was Russell's remit from the Board and shareholders that he employed any suitable method to turn the ailing fortunes of Fairchild around.

Fairchild's produce a range of kit cars based on Vauxhall running gear. They manufacture and supply body shells and components to customers, who then purchase and use Vauxhall engines and parts and assemble the cars themselves. Though they were always relatively popular in the kit car market, Fairchild's never had a high enough production and sales level to warrant mass production techniques or becoming a PLC.

However, increasing labour and raw material costs forced Fairchild's to raise their prices to maintain profit levels. This resulted in a fall in orders for Fairchild's cars. It was in an attempt to overcome this situation that Russell Freemantle was appointed by the private limited company's board to change the situation.

Russell's first recommendation was to float the company on the stock exchange, generate sufficient capital to invest in more automated production, reduce the cost per unit of production and expand demand for the product. Russell successfully managed to float the company and then proceeded on his radical development of Fairchild Motors PLC. Confident of his continued success Russell introduced change as he saw fit, brushing aside the traditional paternalistic management style and adopting an autocratic approach towards other directors and employees alike.

Now, five years on, the Board has recommended that Russell be given a generous golden handshake and that he and the business part company. The board is grateful that Russell has managed to turn the fortunes of the company around, even to the point of launching and developing a single model racing series for Fairchild 380 model cars. However, the board are concerned about increasing labour turnover figures and they, collectively, believe that Russell's management methods are too old fashioned for a forward-looking manufacturing concern.

Recent developments in other larger vehicle manufacturers have also proved interesting to the current board and they are keen to explore some of the perceived benefits of a more democratic management style and the adoption of more modern techniques like quality circles or Management By Objectives.

Question to try

(a) Differentiate between the terms 'autocratic management' and 'paternalistic management'. [6 marks]

(b) Outline two benefits to be gained from a business having an autocratic Managing Director. [6 marks]

(c) Analyse the advantages and disadvantages of introducing a Management By Objectives system at Fairchild's. [8 marks]

(d) Evaluate the actions a business may employ when faced with a situation of high labour turnover. [15 marks]

Answers can be found on pages 99–101.

Exam Question and Answer

Needing bottle, changing production

Spratts Bottles, established 1867, is one of the UK's oldest manufacturers of screw cap bottles. For the last 50 years they have relied upon a mass production line technique to manufacture their four standard size bottles. They then supply to customers as per their individual requirements. Ten years ago they revamped all their production lines to manufacture 500ml, one, two and four litre size bottles.

Several recent developments have started to cause the Spratts management some concern.

- More and more of Spratts customers are moving over to JIT methods of stock holding. This means that at the times when several orders are received at once, Spratts struggle with capacity. The obvious answer is for Spratts to stockpile. However, their warehouse space is limited.

- The move to metrication of all retail quantities has meant that Spratts now face extreme competition from producers all over Europe. Metrication also means that the variety of bottle sizes and customers is now much greater. Hence Spratts themselves are being forced to re-tool and redesign their own products and they must be able to offer a much more flexible service.

Spratts' management team are determined to see their current situation as an opportunity rather than a threat. They realise that the pressures upon them to change their traditional working practices could be used as a vehicle to introduce more efficient production methods. The management has asked members of the production line teams to put forward ideas about how production for the new designs could be approached in terms of factory layout, working conditions, products and production methods. The management sees this as their first step towards introducing lean production techniques and closing the productivity gap that exists between themselves and some competitors.

As an additional service, Spratts are able to provide their customers with labelling and bespoke bottle caps. However, they often just ship blank empty bottles direct the customer's own filling plant. This means that the staff who work in the tailored label and cap production have considerable periods of idle time followed by peak production when orders are received. The fluctuating utilisation of this aspect of the business means that this additional service is consequently operating on a very small profit margin. Frequently customers who desire labelling and capping services purchase Spratts' bottles, but then ship them to alternative suppliers who can offer a more competitive price for the finished details. Spratts are loathe to lose the ability to offer customers this extra service but along with the other proposed moves the management is keen to streamline operations and reduce waste. One of the current proposals is that Spratts look to subcontracting this area of their operations. Management has identified that this would also provide the possibility of greater warehouse space or alternatively increase productive capacity of bottle manufacture by 18%.

Spratts therefore see this whole situation as an opportunity to increase their productivity and hence competitiveness in the EU bottle market.

(a) What is meant by the term 'productivity gap'? [2 marks]

(b) Outline **two** benefits a company like Spratts may gain as a result of subcontracting part of their operations. [6 marks]

(c) Explain the advantages the company might expect as a consequence of expanding productive capacity by 18%. [6 marks]

(d) Consider the Spratts management's motives in asking production line teams for their ideas. [8 marks]

(e) Examine to what extent productivity is the main determinant of a firm's competitiveness. [15 marks]

LEE'S ANSWER

(a) What is meant by the term 'productivity gap'? [2 marks]

The term productivity gap refers to the gap in production between two firms. It is the gap or difference between the amounts that the two companies produce.

$\frac{1}{2}$

How to score full marks

- Lee's answer in the first sentence is **a classic error. All he has done is to re-order the words in the question.**

- The marks available for this question would be split into two levels: **level 1 for some understanding** and **level 2 for good understanding.** Here Lee **shows a little understanding** and so would gain one mark.

- The second sentence does add some more detail by stating it is the difference in the amounts produced. **To gain full marks when defining business terms you need to be specific.** In this case, to gain both marks, Lee needed to say 'a productivity gap is the difference in efficiency with which two rival firms turn inputs into outputs'. It is not just the amount produced since one firm may be much larger than the other. **The focus is on the efficiency of production.**

- **In this question it would be very difficult to give a clear example** and you can tell that one is not expected because the question is only worth two marks. This highlights the usefulness of **structuring your answers to the number of marks available.**

(b) Outline **two** benefits a company like Spratts may gain as a result of subcontracting part of their operations. [6 marks]

Subcontracting operations can bring several benefits to a firm — in Spratts' case, by subcontracting the printing of labels and caps operation. It allows them still to be able to offer their customers this service, so they won't lose any customers whilst at the same time maybe being able to offer it at a lower price. It is likely that the subcontractor will specialise in this area of operations and so be able to do it at a cheaper price than Spratts currently can. Spratts can either absorb this differential in the form of higher profits or pass this cost saving onto the customer and maybe attract more custom as a result.

A second benefit could be that this means Spratts don't need to employ staff who stand idle some of the time. This will save the business costs of wages and overheads incurred from their employment. This would therefore lead to lower business costs overall and again the ability for Spratts to offer either lower prices or receive higher profits, as they would no longer be employing expensive staff to stand around doing nothing. Alternatively these staff could be used more effectively in bottle production elsewhere.

6/6

How to score full marks

- For a question such as this that asks you to **'outline'**, the examiners are looking for an explanatory answer. Hence the mark scheme for this question would appear as: **Content 3, Application 3**. The top level of each skill would be awarded for **a good answer that was in context**.

- Lee's first paragraph is correct: he has assessed the data and put forward a well-reasoned argument of a possible benefit. The main highlight of Lee's answer is **that it is not a purely theoretical text book answer but one that applies directly to the firm in the question**. This enables Lee to generate good marks for application or putting his response in context.

- In his second paragraph, Lee uses a more conventional approach by outlining a possible benefit that could be applied to any business. Again his response is very good as he **discusses why, where and how the actual benefit would occur**. This is the perfect way to move through the levels of response.

- At this point Lee has gained the full marks: **Content 3, Application 3**.

- Another major plus point is that Lee has avoided giving the obvious answers that were presented in the text of the question itself – the ability to turn the space saved into extra warehousing or production space. Although these are also benefits, the examiner would regard them as **just repeating text from the case study. They would therefore be worthy of only very low marks**, unless very well presented and thoroughly discussed.

(c) Explain the advantages the company might expect as a consequence of expanding productive capacity by 18%. [6 marks]

The first major advantage Spratts could achieve as a result of increased capacity is that they would be able to produce more products. However, in order to do this, Spratts would need to purchase more machinery and perhaps hire more staff. These would cost Spratts quite a lot — both to purchase machinery and to train new or existing employees in its use.

Their increased ability to produce bottles, though, should mean that they benefit from economies of scale. For example, the increase in raw materials needed to meet the extra capacity may allow Spratts to benefit from cost savings due to bulk buying. This in turn would allow them to either have a more competitive price or perhaps a greater profit margin.

4/6

How to score full marks

- 'Explain' means the examiners are looking for you to **demonstrate both knowledge and development**. As in the previous question, the mark scheme would be: **Content 3, Application 3**.

- This is an answer of varying quality. Lee has written very fluently on this matter but in the course of his response he has **lost the focus of the question**. This is demonstrated in paragraph one where, although **Lee's response is correct, it is not an advantage**. He would receive just one mark for stating this simplistic point (that is, it would mean Spratts could actually produce more).

- The second part to this answer is spot on. In this section **Lee has presented a valid benefit that may occur**. Furthermore, Lee has developed the point about economies of scale by explaining **how** the benefit might be gained. Lee has used an example of a purchasing economy of scale. He could also have used arguments involving managerial, financial or technical economies as completely separate arguments to generate very good marks. One of the best points to consider from this answer is that Lee, unlike many students, **has not made the assumption that this benefit would be automatic**, he has outlined a **possible** benefit.

- Further lines of approach could have included the ability to spread existing fixed costs across a greater output, so reducing the cost per unit, or alternatively the idea that Spratts may have been able to introduce a wider range of products using the increased capacity.

- Lee loses marks for failing to put his answer in the context of the company or scenario. This could have been achieved by referring to their need, at times, to stockpile in order to meet future production. Lee would achieve: **Content 2, Application 2**. Total 4.

(d) Consider Spratts management's motives in asking production line teams for their ideas.

[8 marks]

The most likely reason that the management has asked for the ideas of the production line workers is that Spratts are about to introduce many new methods of working. This is because they are about to change from their more traditional production to a more lean approach and re-model their production lines. The management of change can be a very tricky problem and as Spratts management have said that they want to 'streamline operations and reduce waste' the workforce may see this as meaning redundancies and job losses or, at the very least, a change and break-up of existing work groups and working methods.

This can be very de-motivating for employees. Maslow's hierarchy of needs identifies security as being one of the lower order motivational factors. If this is removed Spratts may start to suffer from decreased productivity and lower quality production as de-motivated staff concentrate less upon their given tasks and perhaps start to be increasingly absent from work. This is also supported by Hertzberg's two factor theory and also by other motivational theorists who all agree that job security is the main motivator.

By discussing the changes with their main shop floor employees, management can counteract these de-motivational effects. By having the chance to put forward their ideas, workers may benefit from higher order motivational factors such as a sense of achievement and recognition and hence not become de-motivated. It also helps to develop communications between workers and managers.

6/8

How to score full marks

- The mark scheme for an analytical question like this would be: **Content 2, Application 3, Analysis 3**. Lee's six marks were awarded as: **Content 2, Application 2, Analysis 2**.

- Lee has employed a useful technique to answer this question. **He has actually applied his knowledge of human resource management to answer a question on operations management**. This is a perfectly valid approach to take. Business Studies is an integrated subject and if you use sound, logical business theory from any topic area, you will gain marks if you apply it properly to the context of the question.

- Lee does not score full marks because there are some weaknesses in his answer. **The first two sentences just repeat the text and as such gain no marks**. The second half of the first paragraph is relevant but does not directly address the question of **why** the management have acted in the way they have.

- Paragraphs two and three do go on to develop this point in depth. Lee applies good knowledge of cause and effect factors backed up with a solid use of theory, Lee has used Maslow's hierarchy of needs to support his answer exceedingly well and he has targeted his answer to the question of **why the management may have acted in this way**.

- **Try to avoid sweeping statements**. In paragraph two Lee has said 'This is also supported by Hertzberg and other motivational theorists who all agree that job security is the main motivator'. This is not true. A good, succinct and to-the-point answer can easily be spoiled if you make the examiner unsure of your actual knowledge.

- Finally, although quite a lengthy response, **Lee has only addressed one point** – that of management of change. **His second relevant factor – that of improving communications – is not developed at all**. If Lee had said that this could aid in introducing the new methods and so help reduce costs, or perhaps improve industrial relations for the future thus reducing the risk of any industrial action associated with the change, then he would have gone on to score maximum marks.

- **Other relevant factors could have been explored**. The shop-floor workers may well have been able to make suggestions about design and layout and production technique that could increase productive efficiency and reduce costs. Involving production line employees in the decision-making process would encourage them to take ownership of the ideas whilst encouraging a more participative approach, again with the view to increasing motivation.

(e) Examine to what extent productivity is the main determinant of a firm's competitiveness.

[15 marks]

A firm's competitiveness can be determined by many factors. Some of the main ones are:
- The price — the cheaper this is, the more competitive they'll be.
- Quality — if quality is poor the business will be less competitive.
- Motivation — to work well a business needs motivated workers.
- However, the more productive a company is the more competitive it should be.

Sorry ran out of time.

 3/15

How to score full marks

- The marks for a 15 mark evaluative question would be given as: **Content 3, Application 3, Analysis 4, Evaluation 5.** Notice the marks are weighted towards the higher order skill of evaluation.

- Obviously **Lee has not left enough time for the final part of this question** and so attempts to gain marks quickly by mentioning as many factors as he can think of in the time remaining. Lee has opted for completely the wrong approach.

- **Levels-of-response marking means that you receive more marks as your arguments develop depth and demonstrate understanding of business relationships.** (See page 8.) Lee's list is all relevant material but there is only brief and limited development of each point. This makes it extremely hard for Lee to get past level one on any of **application, analysis or evaluation.**

- **If you run out of time, you are much better off developing an argument on one point, rather than listing lots.** If Lee had done this, he would have gained at least a few more marks by moving through to level two on application and analysis.

- Technique is important. Lee's first sentence is an introduction and contains no content worthy of merit; similarly neither does writing an apology. This is all valuable time that could have been used to gain marks. **The way to approach this question is to provide a balanced argument** giving reasons why productivity is important in achieving a competitive position, that is lower costs perhaps leading to lower prices. Then discuss factors that oppose the view that productivity is the most important. For example, develop the argument that in some markets, quality is the most important factor that leads to sales. Perhaps in a more international market such as the one Spratts operates in, it may well be factors like interest rates and exchange rates that actually determine their competitive position.

- A key point to remember here is that in many markets, price is not necessarily the most important factor.

- For this response Lee only scores: **Content 3, Application 0, Analysis 0, Evaluation 0.** Total 3 for giving a series of relevant points.

Don't forget ...

Make sure you leave enough time to answer the final question, as this will usually be worth the most marks. You don't have to answer questions in the order that they are set. The final **evaluative** part will often be worth up to 33% of the total question. By leaving insufficient time to answer you are severely limiting your chances of a high overall grade.

Although this question is about operations management, don't be afraid to draw on other areas. In part (c), for example, Lee used a good, well-developed human resource argument to gain 75% of the marks available.

Use the information given in the scenario as a prompt to help you. For AQA candidates, there will always be two scenarios per data-response paper. Don't be afraid to use relevant ideas from one scenario to help you answer the other.

Stay focussed on the question, particularly questions with higher mark allocations. Students often become wrapped up in their own arguments and actually forget the question they're meant to be answering. **Re-read the question after each paragraph you write so you stay focussed**.

Don't use bullet pointed lists or a plan layout when trying to gain marks if short of time. Usually an extended piece of prose will take less time to write and gain you more marks as you develop a relevant point and move through the response levels.

Always refer to the circumstances of the business or situation you have been presented with. Marks are available for context or application. It makes achieving higher order evaluation marks easier as you can then make a specific reasoned judgement about the most important areas that influence or impact upon the scenario given.

Keep up-to-date with business issues in the media. Business Studies is a real-life subject. Theories are actually developed and applied by managers every day, so being able to select and use a real-life example to add weight to your responses will **help boost both your understanding** of the business world, **and consequently your grades as well**.

Presentation is important. All examination papers now carry marks available for quality of language. These assess your ability to use terminology and language clearly and appropriately. In particular, the use of well-structured paragraphs is a good way to demonstrate to the examiner that you are about to discuss a new point or employ a different examination skill, for example, you have now moved from analysing to evaluating.

Productive efficiency

- The objective for a business is to maximise its outputs with the minimum of inputs. This is what is meant by **productive efficiency**. By improving efficiency, the costs of inputs such as labour or capital can be reduced or output can be increased. Lower prices, better quality and higher profits could all result.

- Another term for efficiency is **productivity**. The most common measure is **labour productivity**, which is measured as output per worker. A productive workforce is likely to be well motivated and trained. Production should be swifter or of a higher quality and rates of absenteeism and labour turnover are reduced.

- **Capital productivity** is another measure of productive efficiency that reflects the ability of a business to make the best use of its machinery or its financial capital. This could be achieved through training employees to use existing equipment better or more flexibly, as well as by upgrading machinery.

- A firm may hope to increase its productive efficiency by growing in size and benefiting from **economies of scale**. These are the reductions in the average production cost per unit resulting from the benefits of being big.

  - Purchasing economies – negotiating bulk-buying discounts

  - Technical economies – making more efficient use of new technology

  - Managerial economies – making more effective use of specialist staff

  - Marketing economies – spreading the costs of selling over a larger output

  - Financial economies – it is often easier and cheaper to obtain finance.

- If a business grows too large, it can suffer from **diseconomies of scale**. These are the factors that push up unit costs once a business has passed its most efficient size.

  - Communication problems – managers become more remote and motivation levels of the workforce may fall

  - Co-ordination problems – the larger and more widespread the organisation, the more difficult it is to co-ordinate activities.

- In order to maximise its productive efficiency, a firm must make best use of its available capacity. A firm's maximum capacity is the amount of output that it could produce if all available resources were employed 100%. The extent to which it is utilising its capacity is calculated as:

$$\text{Capacity utilisation} = \frac{\text{Current output (per period)}}{\text{Maximum possible output (per period)}} \times 100\%$$

A firm under-utilising its available capacity, maybe because of a lack of demand for the product, is regarded as having **spare capacity**. Spare capacity means that fixed costs are spread over fewer units and so unit costs rise. Under-utilisation of labour results in workers standing idle or being made redundant, thus damaging motivation and productivity. Under-utilisation can be addressed through **rationalisation** (cutting the capacity) or seeking to increase demand and, therefore, output.

- A business is unlikely to run at 100% capacity utilisation for long periods of time as it imposes strains on both workforce and machinery, and leaves the business unable to meet a surge in demand. Every business needs to strike a balance between the benefits of high capacity utilisation and the overworking of its resources, leaving no room for flexibility.

- To remain competitive in domestic and global markets a business must seek the best mix of labour and capital to ensure a balance of productivity and flexibility. Where a business uses a high proportion of workers compared with machines, the production process is termed '**labour intensive**', whilst '**capital intensive**' refers to the predominance of machinery.

Key points to remember

- There are three main types of productivity.

  - **Job production** is often labour intensive, producing one-off items to order. Production is very flexible, tailored to the specific needs of a customer, and so can be a quite expensive and complex process.

  - **Batch production** allows the business to benefit from some economies of scale by using capital to produce a limited number of identical items.

  - **Flow (or mass) production** is a capital intensive method of manufacturing a large quantity of similar goods along a production line. It can be cost efficient but is inflexible in that it produces a standardised product and requires a market with high sustainable demand.

Controlling operations

- **Stock control** is the process by which a business ensures that the stock it requires to operate is ordered, received and allocated efficiently. This can include raw materials or components, equipment or finished goods.

- A traditional stock control model indicates the minimum (**buffer stock**) and maximum levels of stock to be held, the **lead time** from re-order to delivery of stock and the level at which stock must be re-ordered. A firm must seek to minimise any **stock wastage** and can use a system of **stock rotation** (using the oldest stock first) to ensure the risks of stock going out of date are reduced.

- The key decision facing a business is how much stock to hold. Without stock holdings a business may not be able to meet increases in demand and could suffer production stoppages if no stock is available. Yet the holding of stock brings extra costs of warehousing and staffing and ties up resources unproductively. It is a classic example of an **opportunity cost**. A business must find the most appropriate trade-off given its circumstances.

- **Quality** is vital if a business is to be competitive – achieving quality means meeting customer needs. Poor quality goods lead to increased production costs through waste, reworking or refunds, as well as loss of sales through decreased customer satisfaction.

- **Quality control** is a method of ensuring consistent levels of quality by using a process of checks to identify problems during production. These checks can either be made by quality inspectors or by the employees themselves (self-checking). Inspection may be more accurate but will be more expensive, whilst self-checking conveys a sense of responsibility to workers and so can help build motivation.

- In contrast to quality control, the basis of **quality assurance** is that instead of weeding out defective products it should prevent them from even happening – getting it right first time. One example of a quality assurance system is **Total Quality Management (TQM)**. TQM requires the commitment of every part of the business to ensure quality is achieved at every stage of production. Creating a 'total quality' culture can be slow and expensive but should result in motivated employees and satisfied customers.

- Effective systems of quality assurance can be accredited with **BS 5750/ISO 9000** certification – the British Standard and International Standard Organisation award for quality assurance. It is quite difficult and expensive to attain and leads to increased bureaucracy within the firm. However, it can lead to increased sales, especially for firms that deal internationally, as some firms will only deal with suppliers who are certified.

- One way a business can seek to improve the quality of its product is through the use of **benchmarking**. Benchmarking involves identifying best practices in other businesses and seeking to bring their own performance up to this level.

Lean production

● **Lean production** is the Japanese business philosophy of eliminating waste in the production process – using fewer inputs: materials, space or time – to achieve the same output. It includes four key aspects.

■ **Cell production** involves splitting the traditional flow production line into small, self-contained units, or cells. It encourages team-working and helps to empower employees in taking responsibility for the production of their cell. Production lead times can be dramatically reduced and quality can be improved through self-checking within the cell.

■ **Just-in-time (JIT) production** aims to eliminate all activities from the business that add no value to the product. In particular, it seeks to minimise unnecessary costs of stock holding, with stock being 'pulled' through the production process only when it is demanded by the 'customer' – be that the final consumer or the next stage in the production process. To employ JIT manufacture effectively, employees need to be multi-skilled, well trained and flexible.

■ **Time-based management** seeks to reduce the amount of time production activities take. One of the major aspects is simultaneous engineering whereby the various aspects of product development can be carried out at the same time. This enables products to reach their market faster, reducing costs and improving profits, particularly in fast-paced, rapidly changing industries.

■ **Kaizen (continuous improvement)** is a technique that focusses on small but steady, rather than one-off and dramatic, improvements. Kaizen attempts to involve all employees at all levels suggesting and implementing small improvements that cost relatively little to implement but, when taken as a whole, add up to considerable advancement. Through team working and empowerment of employees, resistance to change can be overcome and motivation enhanced. It does not suit every business, however, and is certainly no universal quick fix.

Toying with success

Lee Aldred has just taken over as the Managing Director of Aldred's Action Figures Ltd. following the retirement of his father after forty-seven years at the helm. Although they were a big name in toy manufacture in the seventies, Aldred's have suffered a continual decline in sales and production for the last decade. Lee's father always maintained that customers were prepared to pay for quality and so his standards were extreme, employing quality inspectors across the production line. Aldred's toys are, on average, 120% more expensive than comparable figures imported from the Far East. Although they have a loyal and dedicated customer base, Aldred's have had to continually reduce capacity.

Rather than gradually watch the family firm terminally decline, Lee made the decision to benchmark some of his leading competitors, in particular Hughsishi from Korea. His first actions as MD were to gather the workforce, outline the current problems and the foreseeable future for the company, declare his intentions to prevent the closure of the company and ask for the support of the workforce and unions alike in implementing change to guarantee future employment for everybody concerned.

Lee then took the bold step of contacting Hughsishi direct and obtained permission to visit some of their production facilities in Korea and discuss operations with some of their management teams. Lee has come back to the UK with some interesting material.

The Korean firm employ a JIT manufacture approach whereby every employee focusses on eliminating waste procedures from the production process. This includes improving factory layouts, eliminating high stock levels, multi-skilling employees to reduce idle time and employing Kaizen (continuous improvement) techniques through production teams. Lee was amazed at the volume of output achieved by one of the Korean factories he visited – it was a similar size to his own but had approximately three times the productive output. One aspect that particularly impressed him though, was the quality of the toys that were being manufactured and the quality assurance systems in place. Hughsishi explained to Lee that their consistent high quality was in part due to the use of employee quality circles.

Subsequently, Lee has called another factory-wide meeting to explain his findings to the workforce, outline some preliminary suggestions about adopting some of the techniques and ask for comments.

Question to try

(a) Explain the meaning of the term 'benchmarking'.   [3 marks]

(b) Outline two disadvantages a business may experience from holding high stock levels.   [6 marks]

(c) (i) Explain the term 'quality circles'.   [3 marks]

    (ii) Analyse the benefits that a company might gain from operating a Kaizen system.   [8 marks]

(d) Discuss the advantages and disadvantages that Aldred's would need to consider before implementing a JIT manufacture system.   [15 marks]

Examiner's hints
● For part (c), you do not have to be able to answer part (i) to answer part (ii).
● In part (d) note that the question asks about a JIT **manufacturing** system. This means that a discussion on the relative merits of purely JIT **stockholding** methods would be sufficient to gain low to average marks only.

Answers can be found on pages 102–104.

Motoring forward – a knotty problem

In recent years there have been changes in the motor manufacturing industry in the UK. Car buyers are becoming more discerning and there is increasing competition from an ever wider choice of manufacturers and models. Nationwide, there have been complaints by consumers, and investigations by the Competition Commission have led to fines for some companies, changes in legislation and falling new car prices. This has led to a massive knock-on effect to the depreciation rate and value of the second-hand car market.

In an attempt to even out sales and avoid the August peak, car registration periods have changed. Despite all this, the trend at the moment is for more sales on the grey import market where consumers purchase cheaper new and second-hand cars from abroad. There are reports that many of these 'presumed bargain' grey import sales are actually stolen cars being re-registered through Far East countries and sold on to the UK. The calls for lower car prices in the UK still persist despite the recent cuts. The traditional moguls of the UK manufacturing world have had plenty to contend with.

Within the UK, comparatively high interest rates have been identified as one of the major factors affecting the international competitiveness of British car manufacturers. Several major companies have demanded that the UK join the Euro to eliminate the uncertainty of currency fluctuations on costs, prices and profits and produce a level playing field within the European Union. Calls from much of the secondary sector to the Bank of England have been treated with caution as the Bank of England tries to maintain a period of economic growth and inflationary stability. The Bank of England point out to its critics that the UK's Gross Domestic Product (GDP) is still rising, consumer confidence and spending remain high, (often financed through increased consumer borrowing despite the rate of interest) and that no-one, including those businesses themselves, would welcome the onset of an inflationary period.

However, it is not just the major manufacturers that have been suffering. Based in Solihull near Birmingham, Spencer's have been supplying quality walnut to the motor industry for decades. The wood they supply is grown and harvested in the UK on their plantations based in and around the Wyre Forest. It is shipped to their manufacturing plant where it is treated and cut into thin sheets for use in car finishing. The thin sheets are used to provide the luxury touches to top-of-the-range executive models that have a walnut-finished dashboard and side door panels as well as other small touches. Spencer's only supply the walnut sheets. It is up to the car manufacturers themselves to cut and shape them for their own various makes and models. This has several advantages:

• It keeps Spencer's own capital and employment costs down.

• It allows Spencer's to specialise in a basic product, providing good cost benefits.

• Spencer's are able to trade with any motor manufacturer worldwide.

However, the mainstays of their business have been car plants within the EU and news that Jaguar, Ford and Vauxhall are all to lose productive capacity within the EU has been a major blow to the directors of Spencer's. Although Spencer's do deal worldwide, they find that they are at an increasingly competitive disadvantage with overseas competitors, especially from the major walnut plantations in some of the Baltic countries.

Spencer's are not alone in their concerns. Many companies that act as support services to the motor manufacturers are finding themselves in a similar position and in some areas unemployment has started to increase far above national averages. Calls are being made for the Government to intervene and help support UK manufacturing and local economies. However, the general feeling in the business world is that the less the Government intervenes in the UK economy the better. One of their major concerns is that as the tertiary sector appears to be enjoying a mini boom and house prices rise across the UK, the Bank of England may be considering a rise in the rate of interest to curb inflationary pressures.

Spencer's board are meeting next week to decide upon their best course of action. Possible redundancies and a scaling back of operations have already been discussed. However, the investment in the plantations takes years to be returned and so one of the first agenda items for the meeting is finding possible new customers or markets for their product. The directors have been given six days to come up with ideas.

1   What is meant by the terms:

    (a) Gross Domestic Product   [3 marks]

    (b) Inflation?   [3 marks]

2   Explain two fiscal policy measures the UK government could take to combat inflation.   [6 marks]

3   Consider the reasons why 'feeling in the business world is that the less the Government intervenes in the UK economy the better'.   [8 marks]

4   Analyse the ways in which a rise in the rate of interest may affect Spencer's international competitiveness.   [8 marks]

5   Discuss the possible effects on Spencer's of an inflationary period.   [15 marks]

6   Evaluate the possible implications for a business like Spencer's of a trend in rising GDP.   [15 marks]

AMY'S ANSWER

1 What is meant by the terms:

(a) Gross Domestic Product [3 marks]

(b) Inflation? [3 marks]

(a) Gross Domestic Product means the value of a country's output. It is found by adding together the value of all the production that takes place in a country, in this case the UK, over a period of one calendar year. It is different from GNP as values from abroad are not included.

3/3

(b) Inflation is the term given to prices when they start to rise. If inflation reaches very high levels it is called hyper-inflation.

1/3

How to score full marks

- Short answer definition questions carrying three marks are still divided into two levels of response: **level 1 for demonstrating partial understanding** and **level 2 (2–3 marks) for good understanding**. The best way to obtain the third mark is to give **an example that enhances the definition**, thus demonstrating a high/excellent degree of knowledge.

- For part (a) Amy's answer is absolutely correct. **She has stated what GDP is and continued to qualify her answer by explaining how it is measured** and the time period over which it is measured. This is a very good, almost textbook, definition. She has even distinguished between GDP and GNP, which although probably unnecessary, leaves the examiner in no doubt that she knows the meaning of the term. Here she would gain all three marks.

- For part (b) Amy's response is not so well defined. **She has made a general statement** to begin with, and her second sentence is irrelevant to the question asked. Inflation is a tendency for a **persistent** rise in the general level of prices. The key word here is persistent, that is, it takes place over a sustained period of time. To gain full marks here it would also be necessary to state that alongside price increases there is, therefore, a corresponding fall in the purchasing power of money. In this instance Amy would only receive a level 1 mark.

2 Explain two fiscal policy measures the UK Government could take to combat inflation.

[6 marks]

There are various things the Government can do to control inflation. The first is that they could put up the rate of interest. This has the effect that spending within the economy falls as it becomes more expensive for businesses and consumers to borrow money. Some consumers don't bother buying expensive products like cars or houses on interest. For businesses, investment becomes more expensive if they have to borrow money, so they too may decide to put off investment until they can afford it more easily. This means that as spending declines, there is less demand for goods and so prices fall, reducing inflation. This can be shown with a supply and demand curve.

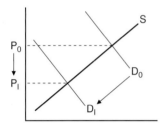

A second way that inflation could be combated is by the Government raising taxation. This could be either direct or indirect taxation, but direct taxation would have a faster effect. Again this has the result of giving consumers or businesses (depending which tax the Government chose) less spending power again, as they are paying more in tax and so have less disposable income to spend at the end of the day. This causes lower demand as shown in the diagram above and prices would fall as demand falls so reducing inflation.

How to score full marks

- In this example, the mark scheme available would be: **Content 2, Application 4**. The question quite clearly states that you need to give **two** measures.

- At first glance Amy's answer appears a sound, well-reasoned response. However, she has made a very common error. **Interest rates are not under the control of the UK Government – they are under the control of the Bank of England** – and it says this quite clearly in the information in the case study. Amy's entire first paragraph is therefore not a valid answer as it is not a way the Government could combat inflation. The major error here is that **Amy has failed to read the case study carefully enough** and so has wasted valuable time constructing an in-depth point worth no marks.

- The second paragraph is a valid method though. Although it follows a similar line of reasoning to paragraph one, it is a valid reason and so does receive marks. Amy has used a good technique here: **rather than drawing the same diagram twice she has referred the examiner back to her previous diagram, to save herself time.**

- As an alternative, Amy could have based a second relevant point around reductions in the Government's own expenditure which would have the effect of depressing aggregate demand within the economy.

- For this response Amy would receive: **Content 1, Application 3.**

3 Consider the reasons why 'feeling in the business world is that the less the Government intervenes in the UK economy the better'. [8 marks]

In many respects, the reasons why businesses feel this are dependent on the way in which the Government intervenes. If the Government intervenes by providing them with grants and subsidies that reduce the businesses' costs and so make them more competitive then I'm sure that those businesses would not be complaining.

However, many businesses see Government intervention as actually hindering their competitiveness, making it harder for them to operate. For example, legislation introduced by Government such as Health and Safety laws or consumer protection laws and the like have the effect of adding to businesses' costs. A good example here is the law on pollution levels. The costs to businesses rise as they have to buy special equipment or introduce new processes to make their products 'greener'. This can be quite good though, as customers and employees may see them as being a more ethical company and hence a company that they want to work for or buy products from. This means that they can improve their reputation or image and thus also increase their sales.

The Government imposes legislation such as the minimum wage on businesses and this legislation does increase costs and so force the businesses to either put up their prices or accept lower profit margins. This then makes them much less competitive.

5/8

How to score full marks

- This question requires demonstration of the skill of **analysis** as **highlighted by the command word 'consider'**. Marks may well be weighted towards this skill and so the mark scheme may appear as: **Content 2, Application 2, Analysis 4.**

- **Amy does consider both sides of the argument.** In paragraph one she writes about the good side of Government intervention. She then follows this up in the next two paragraphs by considering some of the more negative aspects. However, she only gains **Content 2, Application 1, Analysis 2.** Total 5.

- The main reason Amy doesn't score higher marks is that **she does not address the focus of the question** 'that the less the Government intervenes'. Paragraph two is a lengthy and in-depth argument but it is more an answer about the benefits of ethical actions rather than answering the question. Amy does receive some marks for stating that legislation can lead to a rise in business costs but she does not develop this line of argument until paragraph three. **Amy makes the common error of not staying focussed on the question** – letting a line of argument run away with her.

- **To gain full marks Amy needed to write in more depth on the negative aspects of Government intervention** such as increased bureaucracy that restricts innovation and even the products that businesses can sell.

4 Analyse the ways in which a rise in the rate of interest may affect Spencer's international competitiveness. [8 marks]

A rise in interest rates could cause problems for Spencer's because they may find that investment becomes harder as it would cost more, or consumer demand may fall if interest rates go up. Alternatively, the exchange rate may increase so the pound may become stronger in relation to other currencies. This would make UK exports more expensive to overseas customers who, instead of buying UK-produced goods, would switch to cheaper products produced elsewhere. This has the effect of reducing UK companies' sales.

4/8

How to score full marks

- Similar to question 3 on page 61, an example of an eight mark scheme would be: **Content 2, Application 2, Analysis 4**. For Amy's answer she actually scored: **Content 2, Application 0, Analysis 2**.

- Here Amy's main problem is that the arguments she mentioned in her answer to question two, regarding reduced consumer demand or the increasing cost of investment, would be good arguments to use in this question, as both would lead to a loss in competitive position. Having written about these in response to another question, she does not want to write the same thing again so she is now struggling for relevant factors to write about. **She doesn't fully develop these points, so receives no marks for application** and only low level marks for content and analysis.

- Amy's point about exchange rates is reasonably well developed and this is where she gains most of her marks. However, she doesn't get top level marks for analysis as **she has only developed a single point** and has failed to consider that Spencer's position would be made even worse by the fact that imports from their Balkan competitors would also become relatively cheaper to UK manufacturers, thus having a double effect on decreasing sales.

- Finally, Amy has made a serious omission. **She has not put her answer in context.** The question specifies 'may affect Spencer's'. **Amy has given a general theoretical answer only and not applied it to Spencer's at all**, and so receives no mark for application.

5 Discuss the possible effects on Spencer's of an inflationary period. [15 marks]

One of the major problems that Spencer's will face is that as prices go up, workers will start to demand higher wages. This will increase Spencer's manufacturing costs, causing them to either put up their own prices or reduce their profit margins. Alternatively, they could refuse to increase wages but this may lead to industrial relation problems and industrial disputes, perhaps even a strike. Either way Spencer's would find themselves in a more difficult position. Even worse is the fact that the employees of the car manufacturers will be doing the same since inflation affects everybody. If the car manufacturers give in to higher wage demands, (unlikely on past history) this will force up the price of cars meaning less car sales and less business for Spencer's. Alongside this, if people have to pay higher prices for everything else, then they are also less likely to buy a car — again meaning less sales for Spencer's. Spencer's could thus find themselves with increasing wages, industrial disputes and falling sales.

Spencer's costs would also rise due to increased prices from suppliers. However, this is likely to be minimal as Spencer's, as well as being a manufacturer, are also a primary producer so in effect they are their own supplier and they are not likely to put up their own costs. There will be some effect though as they must buy some things, and if their suppliers are also facing rising wage demands then Spencer's will end up paying more for supplies somewhere. This is known as the wage-price spiral, or cost-plus inflation where rising costs push up prices which, lead to higher wage demands, that cause rising costs, that push up prices.

This could again cause increased costs for Spencer's such as 'shoe leather costs' or 'menu costs' because Spencer's would have to spend more time and money searching for cheaper suppliers or updating their own brochures and leaflets with the new prices all the time. However, as many of Spencer's customers are overseas-based manufacturers, a period of UK inflation may have very little effect if there is no change in interest rates or exchange rates.

13/15

How to score full marks

- This question requires demonstration of the skill of **evaluation**. A 15 mark evaluative mark scheme might be given as: **Content 3, Application 3, Analysis 4, Evaluation 5**. Again the marks are weighted towards the higher order skills of analysis and evaluation.

- This is an excellent answer throughout. Amy has made her responses relevant to the case study given. She has picked up and **used key factors from the case study in her analysis**, for example, the fact that the effect on Spencer's is very much determined by the effect on their customers. As Spencer's do not supply direct to a retail market this is an important bit of analysis. Furthermore, Amy identifies that Spencer's is vertically integrated and is also a primary producer. She therefore makes a reasoned judgement that some effects may be minimised. This is an evaluative statement (which this question does require, **highlighted by the command word 'discuss'**).

- Amy then consolidates her answer with good knowledge and application of business theory, outlining the inflationary spiral. **Analysis marks can also be awarded for sound use of business theory**, not just developing points.

- The only reason that Amy doesn't get full marks for a very strong answer is that she **has only considered one side**, that is the negative effects of inflation. Amy would have secured the very top level for **full analysis and evaluation** if she had put forward the following argument: that for companies that borrow heavily, inflation is a good thing as it reduces the real value of any debts outstanding, thus making them easier to repay. Amy receives: **Content 3, Application 3, Analysis 4, Evaluation 3**. Total 13.

6 Evaluate the possible implications for a business like Spencer's of a trend in rising GDP.

[15 marks]

A rising level of GDP in the UK economy would mean that as each year passes there is more output in the economy. This means that, either companies are investing more in training and equipment so they can produce more, or they are directly employing more people. Either way, rising GDP implies more employment in the economy, as the people who do the training or make the machines will have more orders. Rising employment means that there will be more people with jobs. This then means that they have more money to spend, which in turn means they will spend more on purchasing goods, which then means more sales and profits for British companies. Rising profits in turn would probably mean that more people would be willing to invest by becoming shareholders or even opening their own businesses to take advantage of increased sales. This means that with increased money for investment, businesses can become even more competitive than before by having better machinery and better-trained employees.

However, businesses could find that with the rise in employment it becomes more difficult to find employees so they have to start paying higher wages to attract them or keep the ones they have. This would lead to increased costs and falling profit margins or alternatively higher prices and hence Inflation. Also, if a lot of people start their own businesses then there will be more competition in the economy and so some businesses will suffer a decline in sales as customers go elsewhere.

Whether or not a business sees rising GDP as an advantage or disadvantage will depend on the type of market they are in and the product that they sell.

10/15

How to score full marks

- As in previous questions, the mark scheme would appear as: **Content 3, Application 3, Analysis 4, Evaluation 5**.

- Amy seems to be tiring and has **lost the basic structure of using a paragraph for each new point**.

- The first paragraph starts with an introduction that is really textbook knowledge and is worthy of only a few marks as the question does not ask her to explain GDP.

- However, she does develop her points and **relates her line of argument to how rising GDP can improve or decrease a company's competitive position**, which is what the question asks for. This is a good example of an answer that **considers both sides of the argument and remains focussed on the question**.

- **Amy has also realised that her answer must have some form of judgement at the end**. It is here that she loses marks. **She has made a conclusion, but it is a statement not a reasoned argument**. In order to gain full marks here Amy would need to consider the circumstances in which rising GDP would have a positive or negative effect. In this case, the basis is that with more people in employment, disposable income goes up and spending increases. Whether a company benefits or not is therefore dependent on whether they supply income elastic or inelastic products. Amy has found evaluation difficult as she **failed to relate her answer to Spencer's business** itself. Thus she will receive good marks for content and analysis, but will lose out on application and evaluation. This answer would be graded: **Content 3, Application 2, Analysis 4, Evaluation 1**. Total 10.

Don't forget ...

A good technique is to **try to think how might different stakeholder groups be affected** by any situation and then consider their reactions. This will provide you with insight into how the business itself will be affected.

If you feel that a line of reasoning is relevant to more than one question don't be afraid to use it twice. Often the inter-linkages between business variables mean that similar effects will become apparent from entirely different causes.

The information in the case study is there to help you. Not all of it will be relevant to the questions asked. However, **you need to be able to make basic assumptions about the type of business, type of market, number of competitors and possible income and price elasticities of the product.**

Know the meaning of the key command words in the question and look at the mark allocation. These will tell you roughly at what level you need to answer the question and how much depth you need to go into. **This is especially important on the case study** where the level of marks available often make students think they need to write more than they really do.

Make sure you **read the case study carefully**. A good technique is to skim through it once quickly to get the general idea. Then re-read it carefully highlighting important points. **You'll often find that any numerical data in the text is there for a reason.**

For AQA candidates, **the 15 mark questions on the case study exam will always require you to evaluate.** Familiarise yourself with what this term means and how your answer needs to be structured (see pages 6 and 7). **Evaluation relies on reaching a reasoned judgement,** stemming from your own arguments. A judgement that relies on statements or assertion that something is so, will gain few, if any, marks.

To get top-level marks on many case study questions, it is necessary to relate your answers to the context of the business and the scenario given. **Think about how situations would affect the individual business you are given.**

'External influences' questions will almost always have some connection with Government actions. Avoid using political answers or making political statements; pure economic theory will also gain few marks. The focus of the question is always about **how are businesses affected,** and your answers should **look at issues from the business point of view.**

65

Key points to remember

Economic opportunities and constraints

- The way a business operates is affected by the conditions of its own particular 'market'. A market is made up of buyers and sellers and it is the number of sellers, and the ease with which they can move in and out of the market, that affect what the business can do. Where many small firms compete, selling near identical products – **perfect competition** – prices must be kept low, with the most cost-efficient businesses surviving. Where a few large firms dominate – **oligopoly** – non-price competition such as branding and product differentiation tends to develop. In a **monopoly** a single seller dominating the market can act as a price maker, with potential rivals hampered by barriers to entry in the market.

- If there is excess **capacity** in the market, prices will be driven down and businesses may need to diversify into new products or markets, or else scale down operations. Excess demand, on the other hand, provides opportunities for rising prices and profits, but can also lead to increasing competition as new firms seek to enter the market.

- **Unfair competition** can result from pricing agreements between suppliers (a cartel), artificially keeping prices high. This is illegal in the UK and against the interests of consumers. Other examples of unfair competition are market-sharing agreements, where firms collude to remove or prevent opposition, and full-line forcing, whereby in order to stock a manufacturer's most popular lines, retailers have to stock unpopular lines as well.

- The state of the economy can create both opportunities and threats for a business. **The business cycle** will affect the amount of consumer spending in an economy as it moves from **boom** (high levels of output, employment and consumer expenditure), to **recession** and **slump** (falling and then low consumer expenditure with rising and then high unemployment) and then back into an economic **upswing** as spending, output and employment all start to rise. However, not all business will suffer the same fate in each phase. Businesses with inferior products will benefit from increased sales in a recession, whereas luxuries will suffer, and vice versa in a boom. Companies that have a diverse range of products or markets may not be greatly affected.

- **Inflation** (a persistent rise in the general level of prices) can occur during a boom when too much consumer demand chases too few goods – **demand-pull** inflation. Inflation can also be caused by rising input costs, such as wages or raw materials – **cost-push** inflation – which leads businesses to put up prices to maintain profit margins. Inflation causes uncertainty over future prices that can cause consumers to reduce spending, and makes it difficult for businesses to plan ahead. Some businesses may gain from inflation if, for example, they are able to increase their profit margins as a result of rising prices.

- **Unemployment** is at its highest during a slump when there is not enough demand for businesses to maintain previous levels of output and employment. This is **cyclical unemployment**. Unemployment can persist because of a mismatch between the skills of individuals and those demanded by employers. Substantial training costs need to be met by either government or business to close this skills gap. Unemployment can have severe effects on a business, with falling sales revenues causing cash flow difficulties. The need for job losses may damage industrial relations and corporate image, with large-scale redundancies proving expensive.

- **Interest rates** are set by the Bank of England to control inflation. A rise in interest rates makes borrowing more expensive and saving more attractive, discouraging consumers from spending. This helps to reduce demand-pull inflation. In contrast, if inflation is low and cyclical unemployment is the problem, there is scope for a reduction in interest rates. This will encourage consumers to borrow more, save less and so spend more on businesses' goods and services. The debt burden of businesses that have borrowed will also be cut, helping to reduce their overheads.

- The **exchange rate**, the price of one currency in terms of another, is central to the success of international trade. If the pound rises in value (**strengthens**), exports become relatively more expensive to overseas consumers, leading to lower sales. Importers of raw materials or components gain as imports become relatively cheaper, thus improving profit margins. Domestic companies may suffer a competitive disadvantage from cheaper import prices. A falling pound will produce the reverse situation with exporters gaining and importers losing out.

Key points to remember

Governmental opportunities and constraints

- UK and EU legislation is designed to ensure adequate health and safety provision for employees, fair treatment in the workplace, adequate consumer protection and free competition. Laws can help consumers, employees and businesses themselves, but are often criticised for adding unnecessary cost and bureaucracy.

- **Health and Safety** legislation seeks to prevent accidents and discourage dangerous practices in the workplace. The main piece of UK legislation is the 1974 Health and Safety at Work Act, updated in 1996. This obliges employers to provide a safe working environment and employees to observe the safety rules within the business. European directives on VDU equipment, pregnant workers and working hours have all added to the body of legislation in this area.

- **Employment protection** legislation defines the rights of workers both individually and collectively. Laws such as the Equal Pay Act and the Race Relations Act seek to ensure equal treatment of workers, regardless of gender or race. Other legislation sets out the rights and powers of trade unions, stating, for example, that trade unions must provide employers with at least seven days' notice of official industrial action.

- **Consumer protection** laws seek to prevent individual consumers from being exploited by unfair business practices. These state that products must be 'fit for purpose', honestly and accurately described and safe for consumer use.

- **Competition legislation** regulates the power of big business, seeking to ensure that mergers, monopolies and restrictive practices do not operate against the public interest. The 1998 Competition Act brought UK law into line with that of Europe, creating a tougher legal framework enforced by the new Competition Commission. Its job is to curb anti-competitive practices by monopoly businesses that have 25% or more market share. Firms face fines of up to 10% of turnover if found guilty.

Social and other opportunities and constraints

- One of the key current debates in business centres on to whom business is responsible. Some hold that responsibility is only to shareholders – to maximise returns on their investment. Others hold that businesses have a **social responsibility** to other stakeholders such as employees, customers and the local community. Some business owners, such as Anita Roddick, founder of the Body Shop, have a genuine belief in, and commitment to, this stakeholder ethos. Others may weigh up that, whilst acting responsibly toward its stakeholders may incur costs, it can also create many benefits, such as a better motivated workforce or an improved corporate image.

- **Business ethics** refers to the moral principles that might guide the conduct of business decision makers. If a business acts in an ethical way it might reject profit maximisation in favour of benefiting society or specific stakeholder groups. Some businesses, such as the NatWest Bank, have drawn up ethical codes of practice that set out standards of personal and corporate integrity, as well as environmental and social responsibility. There is no doubt that positive publicity of ethical behaviour can create marketing benefits and can help in recruiting and retaining staff. On the other hand, they can be seen as an unnecessary and unsustainable distraction from businesses' primary responsibility of survival and profit maximisation.

- **Technological change** provides further opportunities and threats for business. New products and new production processes can rapidly alter markets, opening up new potentially profitable gaps. New technology in production processes can help to improve quality and increase productivity, but can also generate insecurity amongst workers who fear redundancy or new working practices. Resistance to change from within the workforce may need to be overcome through consultation, security and training. Introducing new technology can therefore be a problematic and expensive process but one that may be essential if a business is to keep pace with its competitors.

Far horizons or rising profits

Smith's, purveyor of vehicles to the military, have recently hit the headlines with a major splash. Having won a large contract with an Eastern government to supply jeeps, trucks, transports and amphibious vehicles for a re-equipment of their land-based forces, Smith's then proceeded to draw up and submit plans for a new manufacturing complex. Although, not very well known outside military circles, Smiths have built up a solid reputation for supplying a range of quality, durable and versatile vehicles. They have been supplying the British and American forces since the Second World War and more recently have generated a good reputation throughout the Middle East. This has come at some cost to the company, however. A prolonged and extensive promotion campaign involving arms shows, exhibitions, trade fairs and entertaining foreign representatives at field demonstrations is only now starting to pay off.

The new contract, won with the help and support of the British Government, guarantees 400 jobs at Smith's existing plant in County Durham and creates 250 new posts for at least the length of the contract, estimated to be five years. However, not everybody is entirely happy with this new development.

Local residents at Harford by Wetton, the village near to the proposed site, have mounted a campaign to try and prevent the proposed factory from ever going ahead. Although, not currently legislated for, the residents of Harford claim that the new site is in an area of outstanding natural beauty with many species of wildlife that need protection. The 'Keep Harford beautiful campaign' first attracted coverage in the regional County Call newspaper. Since then it has picked up national press coverage and is actively being supported by the Friends of the Earth. Alongside their claims of natural beauty, the residents claim that the new factory would also bring noise and environmental pollution to the area. A spokesman for Friends of the Earth levelled criticism at the Government for 'mouthing environmental platitudes without effective controls' and accused them of 'promoting profits over people'.

Smith's, aware of the potentially damaging effects of national news coverage, assured residents that they had a longstanding environmental policy and ethical approach to business and that Smith's would undertake public investment in the local area to help promote prosperity and a community partnership. However, they also maintained the current proposed site was ideal in terms of location for workforce, infrastructure, co-ordination with the existing site, privacy and cost of construction. Residents though, believe that Smiths have failed to take into account the social costs such a site will bring with it to their community.

An unfortunate side effect of all this is that Smith's have now come to the attention of pressure groups like Greenpeace, who claim that the building of such a factory to fulfil the obligations of an obviously unethical contract mean that Smith's cannot be trusted and so any or all information given out by Smith's about the site should be dismissed. The three pressure groups now involved have formed a joint force to lobby the Government to reverse the permission for building the new site and intervene in the granting of exporting licences to Smith's that enable them to supply Far East non-democratic governments with military weapons.

Question to try

Smith's have mounted their own campaign, focussing on their ethical responsibility to their existing employees and families as well as the benefits of job creation and community investment in an area of high unemployment. Smith's also maintain that they have acted with an ethical business policy, alongside Government support and assistance throughout their negotiations and that they don't require a more ethical approach, as they believe their current business ethics surpass those as laid down by the British government.

1 Explain the meaning of the terms:

   (a) Business ethics   [3 marks]

   (b) Pressure group.   [3 marks]

2 Explain two courses of action Smith's may have pursued when faced with pressure group activity.   [6 marks]

3 Examine how the UK Government could have supported and assisted Smith's throughout their negotiations.   [8 marks]

4 Analyse the policies available to the UK government in controlling the extent of Smith's environmental pollution.   [8 marks]

5 Discuss the extent to which an ethical business policy will affect Smith's profits.   [15 marks]

6 To what extent should businesses operate in a more environmentally friendly manner?   [15 marks]

Examiner's hints
- For question 2, you do not need to develop an analytical answer. The command word says 'explain' only.
- None of the above questions ask you to discuss or comment on whether or not you think Smith's is right. They ask you to apply business knowledge and theory to assess a given situation, looking at advantages and disadvantages, pros and cons and arriving at a judgement.

Answers can be found on pages 104–108.

6 Objectives and Strategy

Exam Question and Answer

Business blues

As with many great inventions, Nigel Jones' ideas came about due to a pure dissatisfaction with the products that were currently available on the market. Nigel graduated in Geography from Wolverhampton University and embarked upon an impressive career in sales, working for a major name in the soft drinks industry. However, one year after the birth of his daughter, he decided something had to be done about the lack of suitable devices to prevent her from getting into cupboards and other places which were not safe for her.

Nigel came up with some ideas that he thought would work and, as he was not a particularly skilled draughtsman, he asked a friend to make schematic drawings for him. Using his business experience, Nigel realised that none of his ideas would ever come to fruition if they were not cost effective. He deliberately tried to keep each idea simple and to use easily available materials. He also produced rough cost estimates for a limited production run of each of his ideas.

When he was satisfied with his results, Nigel's next step was to consult with a commercial lawyer and get his ideas patented. Having done this, he then approached major retail outlets with his designs in an attempt to win a contract that would help finance the initial production cost. Unfortunately, their response was that Nigel would have to prove his ideas were successful and marketable before any of them would offer a contract. Undaunted, he approached some manufacturers with the intent of selling his ideas to them. However, the response was the same.

Nigel was convinced that his ideas were genuine profit makers and so he took the next big step. He convinced his family to invest some money, prepared a business plan and set up his own business – in a small way at first. He started by contacting small independent outlets and convincing them to take his products on a sale-or-return basis, with the vendor receiving a commission for each one sold. Within eight months orders were flooding in and 'Baby Friday, make every day a good day' products were in demand and sale-or-return was replaced by direct sales to retailers. Soon after this the company underwent its first expansion and Baby Friday became Baby Friday Limited.

Five years down the line and with a far greater range of products Nigel, now Managing Director, and the rest of the board discussed the idea of opening their own retail outlets and maximising their profits. However, limited capital and already high gearing due to further expansions and investment in production capacity, meant that pouring money into starting a chain of retail outlets was not a viable proposition at this time. A part of the discussion even considered the idea of franchises, but this too was rejected as being to costly to set up. At this point Nigel realised that although his products had become a success he had no idea as to what direction his company, now with a turnover of several million pounds a year, was heading.

Nigel decided to call an open meeting and invited the board of directors, shareholders and employee representatives from the various departments. His aim was to gather preliminary ideas and viewpoints about the company from which Nigel could draft the company's mission statement and develop a set of corporate aims and objectives. However, things didn't go according to plan. From the outset, when Nigel asked for comments on what the various parties believed the business was trying to achieve, arguments started. Nigel was horrified to find so much conflict between some of the different stakeholder groups in the company.

1 What is meant by the terms:

   (a) Stakeholders   [3 marks]

   (b) Franchises?   [3 marks]

2 Outline two benefits Nigel may have received from patenting his ideas.   [6 marks]

3 Explain three benefits a business may gain from becoming limited.   [6 marks]

4 Consider how a business plan may have helped Nigel in setting up his own business.   [8 marks]

5 Examine the possible advantages the company might expect to experience from having a mission statement and corporate aims.   [8 marks]

6 Discuss the extent to which differing stakeholder groups may have conflicting aims.

                                                                    [15 marks]

JON'S ANSWER

1 What is meant by the terms:
   (a) Stakeholders   [3 marks]
   (b) Franchises?   [3 marks]

(a) A shareholder in a company is someone who is a part owner of that company. They have purchased a right to participate in the profits of the company. An example could be ordinary or preference shares.   ⊘/3

(b) A franchise is a type of business operation which is based on the licensing of an already successful business idea. The franchisee pays the franchisor a fee or part profit share in order to obtain the right to use the franchisor's products as their own. Good examples of franchises include McDonalds and Tie Rack.   3/3

How to score full marks

- For part (a), Jon's answer contains factually correct information but he has made **one of the most common mistakes** on Business Studies papers every year. In his haste, he has misread 'stakeholder' for 'shareholder'. This is very easy to do, so when you see either of these terms make sure you double check which one it actually is.

- For a three mark definition such as this, Jon obviously scores no marks for level 1 or 2, as his answer is incorrect. However for part (b) Jon has shown a good example of how to respond to this question with a **developed description and suitable example**.

- A stakeholder is regarded as being any individual or group that has a direct interest in, or is affected by, the performance and activities of a business. Examples include employees, shareholders, customers, suppliers or government.

- For part (b), Jon has defined the correct term and offered a briefly expanded explanation. Alongside this **the inclusion of two relevant examples reinforce** his response so he gains full marks.

2 Outline two benefits Nigel may have received from patenting his ideas. [6 marks]

By patenting his ideas Nigel becomes the only person who is legally allowed to use those ideas for commercial gain for a protected period of time. This allows him to benefit from his inventions by being the only person who can earn an income from selling them. This means he could either make and sell the goods himself without fear of being copied, allowing him a monopoly on these particular designs, or he could sell or license the designs to someone else and earn money from a one-off payment or royalties. Also, by patenting his ideas, he reduces the risk factor of setting up his own company, as he knows he will have a product with a unique selling point as no one else is allowed by law to produce it. This in some respects helps to make sure the business will be a success as, although there will still be competitors, Nigel will have some degree of protection. The USP features of his products will also help him attract sales as these can be used as promotional points to attract consumers.

6/6

How to score full marks

- The likely mark scheme for an explanatory question requiring two definite points is: **Content 2, Application 4**. In this case, Jon easily scores full marks for his considered response.

- **Jon's answer focusses entirely on the question.** His response describes in detail the benefits that can accrue from having patented designs. The key factor here is that he explains why patented designs would be beneficial in the context of someone thinking of setting up their own business.

- The only other points that Jon could have mentioned would have been that with patented ideas Nigel may have found it easier to attract investors because of decreased risk. A further benefit is that when someone applies for a patent, the Patent Office conducts a search of existing product ideas. This allows an applicant to know for certain whether or not their ideas are truly original. If similar products are already in existence, a patent will not be granted. The applicant, who thought they had an original idea, thus does not waste more time and effort trying to launch a product that already exists.

3 Explain three benefits a business may gain from becoming limited. [6 marks]

The first and perhaps most significant benefit that could be expected is that the company would now benefit from limited liability. This means that the personal assets of Nigel and investors are protected. If the company does liquidate all that the shareholders would lose is the value of their investments in the company. This makes it much easier for limited companies to attract investors, as they are able to offer a less risky investment than, say, an equivalent sized partnership. Similarly, as there is less risk involved and more people are willing to invest, this allows the business to raise more capital. This in turn allows them to purchase better machinery, or benefit from a more secure cash flow as they have higher initial working capital levels. Alongside this, more capital may mean the possibility of spending more on better marketing campaigns, attracting a wider base and larger quantity of customers. A final advantage would be that limited companies have a separate legal identity from their owners.

6/6

How to score full marks

- Although this again is an explanatory question, as the response here requires three points, the mark scheme is likely to be: **Content 3, Application 3.**

- Jon's writing style leaves room for improvement – **he does not**, for example, **start a new paragraph for each point that he makes** so it is harder for the examiner to follow his argument. This will not affect his marks for this answer although it **may affect his marks for quality of language at the end of the paper.**

- Jon has developed the points of limited liability and additional capital very well. In fact, this is a **clear case of over-development** as the command word for this question only asked him to 'explain'.

- Unfortunately, the third benefit that the question asked for has been added as **a statement with no further development and this is where Jon could lose marks**. Jon needed to expand on this point to say that this gives additional protection to the shareholders in case the business is sued for any reason.

- However, in this instance Jon has raised three relevant points and developed two of them extremely well. Although he does not develop the third point, the depth and nature of the rest of his answer still enable him to gain full marks. Thus Jon receives: **Content 3, Application 3.** Remember it is possible to reach the top of any skill level through a single point (if demonstrated well enough).

4 Consider how a business plan may have helped Nigel in setting up his own business. [8 marks]

A business plan could have helped Nigel in setting up his own business as it would have helped him determine whether or not his ideas really were viable. Nigel would have had to think about all the different aspects of the business: market research (establishing if people actually wanted his products and would buy them, and the likely level of demand and how he would market his products), how to raise finance, drawing up forecasted profit and loss accounts and balance sheets. This would give him a good idea of whether or not it would be worthwhile giving up his secure job and starting out in business on his own, by allowing him to estimate how much profit he might make. Nigel would have been able to use the plan to convince others, namely his family, friends and the bank manager, that his idea was a workable one. It would help him to raise more finance than if he had just said he had an idea — especially where the bank was concerned. Again, this would help reduce the level of risk and increase the business's chances of survival as the more money Nigel is able to raise to start his business, the greater the chance it has of being able to market more effectively to attract customers, or to have cash reserves to survive a cash-flow crisis. A good business plan would have included a cash-flow forecast so this would allow Nigel to spot any potential hazards. He could then draw up a contingency plan such as arranging an overdraft facility, so that the business did not fail in its first few months from simple mistakes. The bank manager and other investors are also much more likely to take seriously an investment proposal for a new business if they can see that the person who wants to start the new business is serious about it and is prepared to put time and effort into preparing things properly.

8/8

How to score full marks

- Jon's rather haphazard style of developing his answers makes it somewhat difficult to establish exactly where and when he moves from one point to another. **It would have been much better if he had started a new paragraph for each new point he made – remember to do this.** Because Jon's answer runs on, it is difficult for the examiner to establish when he is moving from just explaining and developing his answer to actually analysing. For a question such as this, Jon needs to demonstrate skills of relevant knowledge, explanation and analysis as shown by the mark scheme of: **Content 2, Application 2, Analysis 4.**

- In this particular instance, **Jon has been given full marks for the simple reason that, in his extended paragraph, he has mentioned every single possible point!** Based on the obvious fact that Jon does understand the benefits to be gained from business plans, he receives just reward.

- Jon's is not a style I would recommend you use. You could try restructuring Jon's response into a **clearer format.** You will probably end up writing less than Jon and stand a better chance of receiving full marks.

5 Examine the possible advantages the company might expect to experience from having a mission statement and corporate aims. [8 marks]

A mission statement and set of corporate aims can provide a sense of direction for everyone in the organisation to work towards. This means that the activities of everyone in the business are all directed towards the same goal. Providing employees with a clear direction and sense of purpose can act as a motivator. Employees who do not know what they are meant to be doing, or why, will often be de-motivated. Motivated employees will be more productive than de-motivated employees. Motivated employees will also take less time off work and labour turnover will reduce. This will reduce the business's costs in the area of sick cover and recruitment cost. Alongside this, employees who are present more frequently will correspondingly be more productive. All this means that the productivity of the business should increase whilst at the same time experiencing reduced costs. This will provide the firm with the definite advantage of a lower production cost per unit and greater profit margins.

A second advantage could be that the co-ordination of activities is better. This is particularly useful in making sure that everybody in the organisation is actually heading in the same direction at the same time.

6/8

How to score full marks

- For an analytical question like this, a common mark scheme would be: **Content 2, Application 2, Analysis 4**.

- Jon has started to answer this question quite well. His first paragraph makes a relevant point and develops it fully. This part of the answer is also a very good example of how **Jon has used his knowledge from the People module to help him answer a question on a different topic area.** This is a perfectly valid and reasonable thing to do. The argument is fully relevant to the question set.

- Jon's second paragraph offers another relevant point but in this instance **there is very little development.** This is probably because Jon finds himself about to launch into the same argument he's just used. He could have developed this point by saying that this helps the business co-ordinate its resources, so that there is no waste or duplication of effort. Again this would help the business save costs and operate more efficiently.

- Other goods lines of approach to this question would include:
  ○ having clear aims allows quantifiable targets to be set so there can be closer monitoring of business performance
  ○ the setting of targets allows Management by Objectives, again providing a source of motivation and co-ordination
  ○ the use of more accurate and effective planning will result in better business decision-making, resulting in lower costs or improved performance.

- A further weakness in Jon's answer is that it is pure theory and knowledge. He has made **no attempt to relate his answer to the scenario and circumstances given.** This makes it difficult for him to achieve top levels-of-response marks for application.

- Therefore for this answer Jon would receive: **Content 2, Application 1, Analysis 3**. Total 6.

6 Discuss the extent to which differing stakeholder groups may have conflicting aims. [15 marks]

There are many different groups of stakeholders within a business. These include shareholders, employees, directors, customers, suppliers, the Government and maybe the local community. All of these groups have different goals that they want to achieve.

- Shareholders want profits so they can receive dividends.
- Employees want higher wages or better working conditions, which would reduce the profits for shareholders, so there is a conflict.
- Directors want to retain profits to make the company grow, so they get paid more for running a larger company. This again conflicts with shareholders' desires for dividends. Directors also might not want to give employees pay rises so they can keep more to make the business grow.
- Customers want cheaper prices or better quality goods for the same price, both of which would mean lower profit margins. Again this conflicts with shareholders' desires.
- Suppliers would also probably want the business to grow so that it orders more goods and they themselves make profits. So they would also want the business to retain profits.

These are just some examples of how stakeholders needs and wants can conflict with one another.

In conclusion, as their needs are always going to be different, stakeholders will always conflict with one another. At the end of the day, though, the shareholders will win as they own and control the business.

8/15

How to score full marks

- Once more **Jon's style has made it difficult for him to achieve good marks.** His introduction contains only a textbook definition and so very limited marks would be awarded for content.

- **The bullet-point approach makes it very difficult for Jon to develop a continuous line of reasoning.** Only Jon's third point comes close to being regarded as analysis. Again his style is restricting his possible grade from the marks available: **Content 3, Application 3, Analysis 4 and Evaluation 5.**

- Jon makes no mention of the opposite arguments although the question asks him to '**discuss the extent to which'.** This opens up the chance for him **to include some discussion of when stakeholder aims and objectives can agree.** For example, if shareholders and directors do respond to the needs of other stakeholders (like customers, employees, suppliers and local communities) then their objective of increased profits may be achieved through higher sales from loyal customers, increased productivity from happy and motivated workers, better relationships with suppliers and less pressure from the local community.

- Similarly, most stakeholders groups would also be happy with the objective of growth – directors receive bigger rewards, shareholders funds are at less risk, employees have increased job security, customers may receive a wider range of products to choose from and the local community has more opportunities for employment.

- **Jon's evaluation is limited in its outlook and thus also limited in terms of levels-of-response,** i.e. it is lacking any substance or depth. A more in-depth evaluation would have made the point that it depends on the ownership of the company. Public limited companies are more likely to face pressures for short-run profits from shareholders than family-owned private limited companies. A final point to have included would be the state of the economy. In periods of boom or upswing the business can afford to invest more in its stakeholder groups, whereas in recession, perhaps all groups will be struggling to have any of their objectives satisfied.

- For this answer Jon only scores: **Content 3, Application 2, Analysis 2, Evaluation 1.** Total 8.

Don't forget ...

For any AS paper 3 examinations: **Arguments drawn from Marketing, Finance and Accounting, People and Operations Management are all valid responses to questions on this paper.**

The focus of Objectives and Strategy questions is always about **how the business in the case study is affected or how it should react.** Your answer should **look at issues from the business point of view.**

The information in the case study is there to help you. In many case studies, there will be supporting charts or table of data. Pay particular attention to these as they may provide valuable clues about market trends, competition or the state of the economy.

To get top-level marks on many case study questions, it is necessary to relate your answers to the context of the business and the scenario given. **Think about how situations would affect the individual business you are given.**

Make sure you **know the meaning of the key command words** in the question and look at the mark allocation. For AQA candidates, the **15 mark questions on the case study exam will always require you to 'evaluate'** (see pages 6 and 7).

Try to remember key areas that may have an influence. Use the mnemonic **SLEPT**: **S**ocial, **L**egal, **E**conomic, **P**olitical and **T**echnological.

It is easier to achieve the higher levels of evaluation if your answer is in context. Applying your responses allows you to make judgements regarding what is the most important or most likely factor for **that business.**

Real-life experience can be just as useful as classroom knowledge. Taking part in Young Enterprise schemes or obtaining literature from banks can be a valuable way of building your insight into Objectives and Strategy problems.

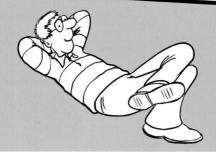

Starting a small firm

● The majority of new businesses fail within the first three years. If this fate is to be avoided, a new business start-up needs to ensure:

■ an **understanding of the market** and the needs of customers has been gained. Even on a small budget, effective research can be carried out into competitors, market size and the views of customers.

■ a potentially profitable **gap in the market** has been identified or can be developed. A new idea or product can then be protected through patents (on products or processes), trademarks (on logos or symbols) or copyrights (on music, art or the written word). Patents prevent competitors from copying the idea.

■ the most appropriate form of **legal ownership** is chosen for the business. At one end of the spectrum lie the sole trader or partnership, where the owners are in control of the business and must personally bear the burden of financial failure (**unlimited liability**). At the other, are limited companies – private or public – where ownership is in the hands of shareholders, who may not have day-to-day control of the business. Here, **limited liability** ensures that shareholders do not have to pay the debts of a failed business out of their personal finances.

■ the **differing resource needs** for starting a manufacturing organisation as opposed to a tertiary organisation are understood. Manufacturing may require a higher level of start-up capital, specialised training or knowledge and reliable sources of raw materials or components. Tertiary businesses, on the other hand, may need to focus on customer service or selling into very competitive markets.

■ the **practical problems of start-ups** are avoided. These can range from insufficient start-up capital leading to subsequent cash-flow problems, to poor business planning, inappropriate choice of business location or failure to build a sufficient customer base.

Legal form	Advantages	Disadvantages
Sole trader	Cheap to form, few legal formalities. Owner receives all profits. Fast decision-making. Able to fill gaps larger business might ignore.	Limited start-up capital and expertise. Unlimited liability. Little support in decisions and no cover.
Partnership (2–20 partners)	A wider range of expertise amongst partners. Greater capital input. Shared decision-making. Cover available.	Unlimited liability. Arguments can occur. Capital input still fairly limited. Profits are shared.
Private limited company	Increased capital through share sales to invited members. Limited liability. Decreased risk. Separate legal identity.	Expensive to form. Must comply with increasing legislation. Unable to sell shares to general public.
Public limited company	Can raise large amounts of capital through share sales on stock exchange. Increased access to sources of finance. Limited liability.	Expensive to form. Must publish accounts. Expensive yearly administration procedures. Pressure on short-term profit performance.

Business objectives

- **Corporate aims** set out the long-term purposes of the whole business and can be crucial in giving that business direction and commitment. A business may express its overall vision using a **mission statement** that sets out the intent, strategy and values of the organisation.

- From the qualitative statements that make up corporate aims come the more specific objectives or goals. These set out what must be achieved in the short- and medium-term if a business is to fulfil its overall purpose. If communicated effectively, these objectives can help to provide the necessary focus, co-ordination and motivation for a business to be successful.

- There will often be a trade-off, however, between relatively short-term objectives necessitated by the circumstances – such as survival in a recession – and the longer-term aims that remain the organisation's ultimate goal, such as becoming the market leader.

- It is also recognised that different groups involved in, or affected by, a business – stakeholders – will each have their own objectives for the business. Stakeholders and their objectives may include:

  - Shareholders – increased profits
  - Managers – business growth
  - Employees – job security
  - Suppliers – prompt payment
  - Consumers – quality and value for money
  - Local communities – care for the local environment
  - Government – creating employment opportunities
  - Financiers – maximising return on investments.

- Their objectives may often conflict, causing poor relationships between stakeholder groups and corresponding falls in communication, productivity, sales and profits, depending which groups are involved. However, stakeholders do share some common objectives such as survival of the business. Stakeholder theory maintains that if the business concentrates on meeting its social responsibilities, then in the long term the desires of all groups can be met.

Business strategy

- If a business is to achieve its objectives it must develop a plan of how this will be done. A business strategy will be based around three key questions:

  - Where are we now? – assessment of its current position
  - Where do we want to be? – setting out the aims and objectives
  - How are we going to get there? – planning the tactics to achieve its goals.

- To understand its current position and how best to develop in the future, a business must understand what it does well (its **strengths**), and what it does not do so well (its **weaknesses**). It must also look beyond its own organisation to its competitive environment, in order to identify potentially positive **opportunities** and more worrying **threats**. This **SWOT analysis** then helps a business to formulate the strategic plan that will use its strengths, build on or remove weaknesses, attempt to maximise opportunities and reduce or remove threats. This should all be done with the corporate aims as a focus for activities. It allows businesses to make informed decisions about how, where and when to allocate its resources in order to meet the objective targets set.

Question to try

Decision time at J & M Taylor

J & M Taylor Ltd is a family run business based in the North East of England. The business is still owned and run by the founders, John and Mary Taylor. Their two children, Robert and Joanne, joined the business after leaving university in 1990 and 1993 respectively. In addition to the four family members, the business also employs twelve other people who are employed in the production of the various products on which the business has built its reputation over the last 20 years.

The business is a supplier of ingredients, such as buns, salads and potatoes, required by the fast food industry. From the start, it has been company policy to supply a large range of products in order that they could appeal to as wide a customer base as possible. This policy has been very successful so far and the company supplies a wide variety of outlets, varying from fish and chip shops to the more fashionable types of outlet, such as tapas bars.

The North East has recently experienced the loss of a large number of jobs in the textile and electronics industries pushing the unemployment rate in the area to approximately 8%. Many people in the region were beginning to economise and were cutting down on any unnecessary expenditure. One of the sectors feeling the pressure from such cuts was the take-away food industry with most outlets reporting a noticeable drop in trade. J & M Taylor was no exception; over the last eight weeks Robert reported a 10% drop in orders from regular customers.

These changes in the local economy have led the family to consider setting up a totally new business that would, hopefully, take advantage of the current fashion for eating organic food. They were considering calling this new venture 'Freshers' and its mission would be to provide high quality snacks using only organic produce. Joanne had been consciously buying organic food whenever she could for almost five years now and was therefore aware of the range of food that was available and its price. She had done some market research and had found that there was not a single café in the area that was offering organic food. Therefore, she was convinced that, although the take-away and café business in the region was seeing a downturn in sales, a new venture promising only pure and wholesome food would attract sufficient people to make the business profitable. Her main problem was that she needed to persuade the rest of the family that setting up a new business at this time was not foolish and was likely to succeed. She emphasised that, although the business cycle was experiencing a downturn at the moment, the family should be prepared for the upturn, which would hopefully follow.

The family decided to hold a business meeting to discuss the options open to them in order to ensure the company's survival. Robert suggested that before the meeting each of them should do a SWOT analysis of the business and they would then have a foundation on which to base their decision.

During the meeting it became clear that they had two main options available to them. Firstly, they could reduce their workforce until demand began to increase again or they try Joanne's idea and start a new business based on organic snacks. They agreed to go away and to meet again in three days when each of them would have prepared a list of advantages and disadvantages of both of the proposals. When they met again Mary shocked them all by saying that she had not bothered to consider the two options because, after leaving the first meeting, she had thought of an even better idea. She said that she was convinced they should concentrate on the business that they have been successful in for the past 20 years and that instead of risking a totally new business they should explore the possibility of exporting products that they make and supply. She argued that the reduction in interest rates made this an ideal time for such an experiment. As Mary had not been known for coming up with ideas in the past, she was rather surprised when John, Robert and Joanne's all agreed that this was something that could be worth considering. Now they had three options to consider!

During the same period that the job losses and the fall in orders were occurring, interest were reduced by a total of 0.75% to 4.25%. This was thought to be in response to appeals from businesses who said they could not afford to invest at the higher rates of interest, and that the exchange rate was being pushed up and was reducing their ability to gain export orders.

1   What is meant by:

    (a) Ltd   [3 marks]
    (b) Exchange rate?   [3 marks]

2   Explain two ways in which a fall in interest rates can affect a business such as J & M Taylor.   [6 marks]

3   Examine the ways in which different stakeholder groups might react to a decision to cut the number of workers in the business.   [8 marks]

4   **(a)** Prepare a SWOT analysis for the business meeting.   [6 marks]

    (b) On the basis of your SWOT analysis, make a fully justified recommendation as to which option the family should choose.   [15 marks]

5   Evaluate the business opportunities for J & M Taylor Ltd resulting from a future upturn in the business cycle.   [15 marks]

Examiner's hints
- Question 4, part (b) is entirely dependant on your analysis for part (a). It is therefore worth spending a little extra effort preparing your analysis. This will help you to maximise your mark for both sections of this question.
- Questions 4, part (b) and question 5 require evaluation, so make sure you include this in your answers.

Answers can be found on pages 108–112.

Ten steps to success

The case study given on pages 82–87 is a recent AQA Module 2 and 3 pre-issued case study. It is being used to demonstrate to you – no matter what specification you follow – a recommended strategy for preparing yourself for an exam based on pre-issued material.

Step 1
Obviously the first thing to do is to read the material presented. At this point, you should have no objective other than to get 'a feel' for the information provided.

ScrewLoose Ltd

A. The End

Looking back, Andrew Couder knew he should have seen it coming. The newspapers had been writing constantly about the recession, yet it seemed to be the big manufacturing companies that made the big staff cutbacks. And, after all, his employer was profitable enough to have just declared a 9% dividend increase to shareholders.

He remembered the Friday afternoon in 1992 when he was called to the area sales manager's office. He remembered seeing a clock showing 3.00 pm as he went in and 3.06 pm as he left. It did not seem long to round off five years' work. Nor did the £5000 redundancy money seem likely to go far.

Yet, could anyone else in 1992 have made such a fantastic investment, he wondered, turning £5000 into £82 000 000 in just 12 years? He reached for the cheque in his pocket yet again. Yes, there it was: £82 million!

B. The Beginning

In 1992, with the £5000 redundancy money in his pocket, Andrew had immediately started looking for a business to run for himself. He never again wanted to be treated as shabbily as he had been by area sales manager, Mr Darnton. But what to do? He looked into starting a Domino's Pizza franchise outlet but lacked the capital. It took him some weeks to stumble upon his new career. It came as he was leafing through Exchange & Mart. His eye was caught by a small advertisement headlined "ScrewLoose?". He saw that the number underneath was quite local, and phoned it. Within two days, Andrew had his new business – *ScrewLoose Ltd*: nuts, bolts, screws and nails by mail order.

To call it a small business might have been an exaggeration. It was tiny. All it consisted of was a rented stockroom with just enough room to pack orders, plus a small office for taking orders and processing them. Andrew had bought the stock, the name and the relatively small list of customers. The fact that it had been sold so enthusiastically for £5000 implied a struggle to make the business pay. Andrew was soon clear on this, as the first month's profit came in at £37.

For two years the business struggled. Andrew hired only one staff member, who took orders, fulfilled them and ran the paperwork system. By the end of the second year, Andrew was ready to quit. It was a boring business to run and still made insufficient profit to give him the income he had previously received as a salesman. Then, with the DIY market starting to recover, Andrew's younger sister, Beatrice, started to show some interest. She needed a topic for her Business Studies A Level project, so she chose to investigate how *ScrewLoose Ltd* might be developed.

She wrote a questionnaire for existing customers and posted it to their home addresses. Once she had a reasonable number of replies, she produced the following summary.

	Are you?	Would buy wider range	Don't want wider range	Want next day delivery	Pay extra for same-day delivery	Want to use credit card	Want credit
DIY	32%	64%	36%	62%	16%	88%	24%
Professional e.g. plumber	68%	84%	16%	92%	56%	80%	68%

This work encouraged Andrew to give the business a last try. He widened the product range and started accepting credit card payments. Both of these changes added to his costs but soon made a significant difference to sales. Quite soon he needed a second employee, then a third.

C. The Take-Off

By 1996, Andrew noticed for the first time that some builders were phoning in their orders while on the move. Mobile phones were still hugely expensive but some builders had them. Within a year, it became rare for any professional to phone on anything other than a mobile. Business boomed.

It was in 1997 that the business hit its first real crisis. The ordering system had always been based on Excel spreadsheets, but the size of the business was outstripping the software. Repeated stock shortages were causing important customers to go elsewhere. Then a move to a big, automated warehouse led to chaos when the Information Technology systems had teething troubles. As more and more customers phoned in abusively, staff quit rather than stay in the firing line.

To his credit, Andrew stayed calm. He wrote a personal letter to all customers (present and past) apologising for the problems and explaining their origins. He got the staff together, explained the difficulties and his planned solution. This helped to stabilise the situation but it remained hard to cope as external factors kept favouring growth. Regular investments in extra stockroom space led to equally regular periods of under-utilised capacity, making it hard to run the business economically. Fortunately, there were increasing economies of scale to keep costs per unit from getting out of control.

In early 1998, Andrew booked a flight to Belfast using the internet. It was the first time that he had done this and he realised that it was incredibly convenient. He had made the booking during half-time in a live television football match and he realised that builders and DIY fans could do the same. The next day he made some phone calls and eventually found an IT freelancer with the skills to build the first *ScrewLoose Ltd* website. Within three weeks it was up and running and by the end of the year it was delivering a lot of new business.

With the technologies of the mobile phone and the internet in the company's favour, sales kept shooting ahead. Andrew could no longer cope. One crisis after another made him ill. When his doctor decreed a one-month holiday, he decided it was time to appoint a Managing Director.

D. Under New Management

CY, as he soon became known to all, had an unusual background as an entrepreneur as well as a manager. Andrew had asked a recruitment consultancy to shortlist five people for the top job, to be ready for his return from holiday. He spent a day with each, taking them round to meet staff, getting them to answer some phone calls from customers and discussing their approach to future strategy. CY seemed the best combination of sharpness, warmth and strategic thinking.

After being appointed in late 1998, CY spent several weeks in further discussions with the firm's key stakeholders. By now, *ScrewLoose Ltd* had over 150 staff, 1000 regular customers and it sold over 5000 different products, so this was not a quick job. When he was ready, he called the staff together and announced a switch to selling via the internet. Staff should, therefore, be able to focus on successful stock management and supply, rather than telephone selling. Many were upset by this but CY's views proved shrewd in 1999 and 2000.

CY's start as Managing Director was helped greatly by the economic circumstances. The housing market was very strong, and when people move house they spend more on DIY. In the meantime, low interest rates were encouraging many to borrow more in order to carry out loft extensions and other building work. Even the exchange rate was in *ScrewLoose Ltd*'s favour, as it was so strong that products manufactured overseas could be imported cheaply.

CY decided that the external circumstances were so favourable that he needed only to focus on the internal workings of the business. He reorganised the number of layers of management by scrapping a supervisory level that seemed unnecessary and adding two other layers further up the hierarchy.

ScrewLoose Ltd, Sales & Profit 1993 – 2003

(For full figures, see **Appendix A**.)

CY was surprised to find how disruptive the changes proved. Staff at the lower levels were furious at the increased workload which they claimed they faced. One grumbled that "a span of control of six is far too many to manage effectively". At the higher management levels, various senior staff were unhappy about the 'loss of face' that they felt if they had been overlooked for a job position with greater status and authority.

Only in one section of the business were there no complaints. The canteen had been opened two years before under the management of Michelle Tia. The growth of the business meant there were now seven people answerable to her, but all seemed very content. CY knew that no member of staff had left the canteen since it opened. He called Michelle to his office for coffee and to ask her to describe her approach to management. She explained:

"I set clear standards, by coming in early, being fanatical about cleanliness and quality and by taking every customer complaint seriously. Then I meet with staff every week to discuss next week's menu and take care to act on staff suggestions, even if I have doubts. Finally, I leave the day's operations to staff, without interference. They know they can call me in at any time to help fill any job, perhaps because someone's been taken ill. I love helping but hate to over-supervise. All in all, it seems to work."

CY decided to take this a stage further by asking a couple of Michelle's canteen staff to come and talk to him. They were astonished by the request and quite nervous, but the meeting went well. They heaped praise on their manager and one quoted as an example:

"One time, I said that we needed a supplier to deliver every two days, not just twice a week. And the supplies needed to be of better quality, especially the meat. Michelle asked the girls to cover for me for a couple of afternoons, so that she and I could talk to some suppliers. Well, it made us all feel good that our manager trusted one of us in that way. Everyone worked a bit harder for a few days and we've all benefited from working with fresher, better quality produce."

CY was very impressed by this and by the evidence that the canteen staff were developing in a way that could make them managers of the future. He spoke to other managers about Michelle's approach, but in some cases it made little impression. The warehouse manager was especially sceptical about "being soft with staff". He believed that staff needed "clear instructions and tight monitoring". "How else," he continued, "can we meet the reliability benchmarks we've saddled ourselves with in our ISO 9000 assurance agreement?"

E. The Competitive Environment

Realising that it would take quite a while to persuade all his managers to change their attitudes, CY changed his focus to more immediate issues. *ScrewLoose Ltd's* success was attracting more and more competitors. Many were small and local. CY's response was to allow pricing flexibility by postcode. If a customer account was registered in Manchester postal area M4, sales staff were given the flexibility to offer a discount of up to 30%. This was to combat the effect of the local competitor, Trafford Tools. On a national level, there were also some problems. Retail giants, N&P and Brewers, were both showing an interest in the market and it was clear that they could both squeeze massive discounts from suppliers. There was no question of competing on price against them, especially as *ScrewLoose Ltd's* gross margin was a relatively modest 23%. Fortunately, the big firms' decision-making seemed extraordinarily slow; and while they tested the market in different ways, *ScrewLoose Ltd* kept growing.

With the pound continuing to get higher and higher against the Euro in early 2000, CY decided it was time to buy a foothold in Ireland. The pound's strength helped make it affordable to buy a family-run, Dublin-based mail order business selling a similar range of products. The Irish economy was growing at a dizzying rate of over 7% a year and, although inflation was quite a worry, there seemed to be outstanding business opportunities. Furthermore, there was even less competition in Ireland than in Britain for mail order DIY supplies.

F. Risk of Divorce

By 2000, Andrew was enjoying the fruits of CY's operational success. That year, *ScrewLoose Ltd* made an astonishing profit of nearly £2 million and Andrew was able to take a dividend worth half a million. But during one of Andrew and CY's monthly meetings, towards the end of the year, things started to go wrong. Andrew spent too long talking about his new villa in the south of France, and CY asked himself why he was working so hard to make Andrew richer and richer. CY tackled Andrew on whether he could have a shareholding in the business, but the answer was vague.

CY's response to this was not immediate. He just found himself taking things a bit easier. He decided on a restructuring of management in which there would be an extra layer of management at the top of the business. This would serve to lighten his workload, yet he asked for a large pay rise for himself due to his greater responsibility for more senior managers. Andrew was too busy with the building work on his new villa to take much notice.

The new senior managers were just about in place when N&P launched a huge television campaign to promote its brand-new, door-to-door delivery service for builders and householder DIY fans. The internet address and telephone number were beamed into every household, all with the "N&P guarantee of next-day delivery or your money back". *ScrewLoose Ltd* found itself under attack from a major business with very deep pockets. Fortunately, N&P were offering nothing that *ScrewLoose Ltd* had not been offering already, so few, if any, customers were lost. Yet prices had to be trimmed and the need for 100% reliability became greater than ever before.

When CY heard of the late delivery of an order to a major client, he demanded an explanation from his new Operations Director, yet he still knew he didn't care as much as he used to. Therefore, when, just a fortnight later, a headhunter phoned to offer him a job running a new internet start-up business, with a 25% share stake, he jumped at the chance.

Shocked out of his stay in France, Andrew returned to take full-time control until a new Chief Executive could be found. He was soon sure that the business was top-heavy, with too many senior managers who had too little to do. One, however, he found especially impressive. It was Michelle, who CY had taken care to promote to Head of Human Resources. Andrew decided that, despite her lack of financial and operational expertise, she was the one he wanted as the new Chief Executive. There was no rush, though, as she would take a while to gain confidence in that role. For now, he made her Deputy Chief Executive, keeping himself as Chairman and Chief Executive.

G. Back To Basics

Although 2001 proved difficult, with profit margins slipping, the business coped surprisingly well with the N&P competition. In effect, N&P's TV advertising boosted the whole concept of ordering DIY supplies on-line, to the benefit of *ScrewLoose Ltd*, as the established market leader. N&P established a 22% market share, but *ScrewLoose Ltd* retained a 53% share of a much expanded market.

In 2002, things stabilised as Andrew and Michelle took a firm grip on senior management, slimming it down by delayering and placing a clear priority on delegation and consultation as the preferred leadership approaches for the future. All the directors and senior staff were required to attend a one-week residential training course on People and Operations Today (see Appendix B), which was held at a luxury hotel in the Cotswolds. This seemed to help the business to keep growing through 2002 and to face 2003 in a strong position.

2003 posed new challenges, as a sharp downturn in Ireland led to severe under-utilisation of capacity there. Fortunately, an idea put forward by a warehouseman at a kaizen group meeting provided the answer. *ScrewLoose Ltd* had invested in a large distribution warehouse with up-to-date, robotic stock picking. The warehouseman suggested offering the facilities to other firms on a subcontract basis. The very firm he suggested, a garden equipment hire business, jumped at the chance to hire an efficient stock control and delivery system. This secured the jobs of those at *ScrewLoose (Ireland) Ltd* and made the warehouseman popular with management and staff alike.

In Britain, despite many worries that the housing-market bubble would burst, things kept going. Even in London, where house prices were slipping, the boom in home improvement seemed unending. *ScrewLoose Ltd* kept growing rapidly and very profitably.

H. The End (Part 2)

Then, in early 2004, with Andrew just having announced that Michelle would take over day-to-day management of the business as Chief Executive, N&P dropped the bombshell of offering Andrew the sum of £75 million to buy the business. He thought long and hard about dismissing the offer, but his wife and family persuaded him that he would be crazy to turn it down. His son, who was studying Management Science, showed him an Economics magazine article featuring forecasts which he suggested were an indication of "future economic uncertainties" (see **Appendix C**). Andrew realised that even if he wanted £50 million to start or buy another business (instead of £5000 last time), the family would still be secure for life with the remainder. So he went along to negotiate, managed to push the bid up to £82 million, and signed his business away.

At Andrew's request, Michelle was kept on to run the *ScrewLoose Ltd* division of N&P and it is too early to say whether the purchase will prove to have been an astute move for N&P. For Andrew, though, the ink on the cheque is still too wet for him to be sure of what comes next. A holiday in the villa seems the first priority – after a quick trip to the bank.

Appendix A: ScrewLoose Ltd's Sales & Profit Data 1993–2003

	Sales turnover (£000)	Profit (£000)
1993	80	1
1994	90	4
1995	120	19
1996	310	61
1997	510	55
1998	1450	125
1999	4100	900
2000	12400	1900
2001	37000	2800
2002	75000	8800
2003	135500	13600

Appendix B: Management Training Programme – Executive Summary

Day 1.　Ice-breaker - Blind Man's Buff
　　　　Seminar by Professor R Raymond on the Psychology of Motivation
　　　　Group activity: discussing case examples of motivated and unmotivated staff
　　　　Video: Professor Herzberg: *Jumping for the Jelly Beans*
　　　　Discussion of video, led by Professor Raymond

Day 2.　One-to-one interviews by delegates on each other's leadership style
　　　　Discussion of findings
　　　　Lecture by Dr J Dymott on latest research into successful leadership
　　　　Seminar debating the implications for *ScrewLoose Ltd*
　　　　Go-Kart relay race

Day 3.　Empowerment and teamworking seminar
　　　　Discussion on DTI Benchmark data on the use of quality circles and kaizen
　　　　Our vision – Michelle Tia on the hopes for future staff development
　　　　Video: *Successful Delegation*

Day 4.　Discussion: What have I learned and what will I do about it?
　　　　Presentation by each delegate on "My Plans For Staff Development"
　　　　Discussion on each

Day 5.　Team-based canoeing and cross-country race
　　　　Early dinner
　　　　Speech by Andrew Couder, Founder, Chairman and Chief Executive

Appendix C: Economic Forecast

	House prices (% change in last 12 months)	Interest rates	Euros to the £	GDP growth	Inflation (% change in last 12 months)
July–Dec 2004	+2.2%	4.25%	1.45	2.75%	2.7%
Jan–June 2005	+0.5%	4.5%	1.40	2.75%	2.5%
July–Dec 2005	–2.4%	4.5%	1.40	2.5%	2.4%
Jan–June 2006	–3.8%	5.0%	1.35	2.25%	2.1%

Step 2

It is essential to make sure you understand the basics. Check back through the key points in each chapter to help you here. The easiest way to do this is to read the material again, making a list of any particular **business terms or phrases** used.

It is also a good idea to organise your lists into **particular subject areas** as below. This helps to make sure you have the **knowledge** necessary to tackle the case study.

Key words/definitions list			
Human Resources	**Operations Management**	**External Influences**	**Objectives and Strategy**
Span of control	Capacity utilisation	Recession	Franchise
Delayering	Economies of scale	Boom	Stakeholder
Delegation	ISO 9000	Interest rates	Market share
Consultation	Kaizen	Exchange rates	Dividend
Herzberg	Teamworking	Inflation	Profit margin
Empowerment	Benchmark	GDP	Limited company
Bonus share ownership	Quality circles	Economic growth	
Motivation	Stock control	Stakeholders	
Democratic	Quality assurance		
Chain of command	Subcontract		
Staff development			
Teamworking			
Recruitment consultancy			
Headhunter			
Training (off and on the job)			

Step 3

The next step is to make sure you understand **the development of the business** and the dynamics of the material presented. You should do this by drawing **a time line** of proceedings and placing on it **key events and decisions** as they happen. This will help you **apply theory and order your arguments** in relation to the different situations faced by the business throughout the scenario:

Key Events	Sales £	Year	Profits £	Key decisions
• Andrew buys business for £5,000		**1992**		
	80,000	**1993**	1,000	
	90,000	**1994**	4,000	• Decides not to quit • Undertakes market research • Expands product range • Accepts credit cards
• Increases number of employees	120,000	**1995**	19,000	
• Increased use of mobile phones, encourages sales	310,000	**1996**	61,000	
• Stock shortage crisis • Staff leaving	510,000	**1997**	55,000	• Move to big automated warehouse • Discusses problems with staff

Key Events	Sales £	Year	Profits £	Key decisions
• Advances in mobile phone and internet technology	1,450,000	**1998**	125,000	• Sets up website • Appoints CY
• Strong housing market • Low interest rates • Cheap imports • Increasing competition	4,100,000	**1999**	900,000	• Switch to internet selling • CY scraps supervisory level • CY allows price discrimination by postcode
• Andrew takes large dividend and takes less interest in running business • N&P advertising campaign helps boost *ScrewLoose* sales • CY leaves	12,400,000	**2000**	1,900,000	• Purchases Irish base • Andrew does not give CY a shareholding • Management restructured extra level added • Michelle made deputy chief exec
• Falling profit margins • N&P advertising encourages market growth	37,000,000	**2001**	2,800,000	
• Residential training course • Growth continues	75,000,000	**2002**	8,800,000	• Delayering of management • Move to democratic management style and culture
• Downturn in Irish economy • Under-utilisation of capacity • Kaizen group meetings in use	135,500,000	**2003**	13,600,000	• Listens to employee suggestion and subcontracts warehouse operation out
• Economic forecast produced indicating future economic uncertainties		**2004**		• Michelle appointed chief executive • Andrew decides to sell to N&P
		2004		**Business sold for £82 million**

Step 4

Having developed a good sense of the key terminology and the sequence of events, you should now be able to draw up **basic company and market analysis**. The examples given below are an outline only. You could and should add any important categories/information you want based on the exact case study you are issued with. Knowing all this company background will help you gain marks for **application**, as you are able to relate your answers to the company's circumstances.

Company Profile: *ScrewLoose*		**Market Analysis**	
• **Legal form**	Private Limited	• **Mass or Niche**	Originally Niche now Mass
• **Sector**	Tertiary Mail order	• **Market Size Value or Volume**	37,000,000/53 × 100 = £69,811,320
• **Objectives**	Profit	• **Growing or Declining**	Growing
• **Mission statement**	Not given		
• **Size**	Small/medium in employee terms (150) Large in terms of turnover (£135,500,000)	• **Barriers to entry**	<u>Low:</u> Supplier knowledge needed and website <u>High:</u> *ScrewLoose* benefits from large economies of scale

• Type of structure	Hierarchical (pyramidal) Centralised	• Local, National or international	Mainly national Some international trade (Ireland)
• Product(s)	Range of 5000 different products (Nuts, bolts, screws etc.) No USP except next day delivery	• Competition	Mainly small, local (e.g. Trafford Tools) Two large, national (N&P and Brewers) becoming more competitive over time
• Key stakeholders	Shareholders (Andrew) Competition Employees Suppliers Customers	• Type of market	Originally monopoly e.g. 53% market share in 2001 Now oligopolistic

Step 5

Understanding the major characters will also help you to enhance **application** marks. These are the people who run the business and make the decisions, therefore it is important that you know their strengths and weaknesses.

Key Person 1 profile: Andrew Couder	
• **Position(s)**	Owner
• **Experience**	Five years as a sales representative
• **Method of recruitment**	N/A
• **Personal Objective(s)**	Profit
• **Management Style**	Paternalistic Consults and listens to staff but makes decisions himself

Key Person 2 profile: CY	
• **Position(s)**	Managing Director Chief Executive
• **Experience**	Entrepreneur and manager
• **Method of recruitment**	External recruitment consultancy
• **Personal Objective(s)**	Growth Become a shareholder
• **Management Style**	Paternalistic Discusses issues with staff, but again takes responsibility for final decision

Key Person 3 profile: Michelle Tia	
• **Position(s)**	Canteen Manager Head of Human Resources Deputy Chief Executive Chief Executive
• **Experience**	Started with the firm in 1996
• **Method of recruitment**	Internal promotion
• **Personal Objective(s)**	Promotion and recognition
• **Management Style**	Democratic Delegates authority Listens to employees Organises training programme

Step 6

Now make a list of the **ten most important decisions made by the business or events that occurred**. Then consider the **impact/implications** of these. Was the outcome of these choices **beneficial or detrimental** to the performance of the firm? This type of activity develops your skills of **analysis**, as you have to think through the knock-on effects of decisions and events.

Significant Decisions/Events	Impact	
	Positive Effects	**Negative Effects**
1 Widen product range	More customers More sales	Higher costs
2 Accept credit card payments	More customers More sales	Higher costs
3 Increase in mobile phone usage	More customers More sales Growth	
4 Move to internet selling	More customers More sales	Overtrading, stress
5 Move to automated warehouse	More efficient service Greater capacity	Staff quit Stock shortages Loss of customers
6 Scrap supervisory levels and add management layers	More specialised managerial roles, a specialisation economy of scale	Disruptive and upset staff Widened spans of control
7 Appoint an MD using external agency	Time effective Use of external expertise	Expensive
8 Delayer Management	Save costs Speed up communications	Motivational effects
9 Change in management style and culture	Continued growth Offset some aspects of dolayoring	Cost
10 Sell the business	Consider what responses you might put here. Hint: often you need to look from different stakeholder perspectives.	

This is not a definitive list. For example, you might also want to consider decisions such as to purchase the Dublin-based company or to sub-contract some operations. You need to make your own list based on your actual case study.

Step 7

Another good exercise to undertake is a **SWOT analysis**. This makes you focus on the business' current position *and* possible future situation. Again this is useful for developing **analytical awareness**.

Strengths	Weaknesses
• Market leader	• Poor capacity utilisation at times
• Large product range	• Stock control and stock management
• Recognised brand name	• Poorly structured/continual change
Opportunities	**Threats**
• Expanding market	• Increasing competition
• Use of technological change	• Falling profit margins
• Supportive economic environment	• Changing economic situation

Step 8

Now you need to complete any other exercises you or your teacher might consider useful in making you even more familiar with the material. Here are some ideas:

- Draw an **organisational structure diagram**: you may need more than one if the business re-structures throughout the scenario.

- Makes notes on the **advantages and disadvantages of different approaches and key themes** highlighted by the case study. For example:
  - Centralised/decentralised
  - Private limited company
  - Management styles
  - Production methods/use of JIT
  - Interest rate levels
  - Social responsibility
  - Methods of recruitment
  - Uses of IT

- Make a list considering **major external influences**. Use the mnemonic SLEPT to help you. Look at:
  - **S**ocial change and influence on the business
  - **L**egal requirements faced
  - **E**conomic influences on that type of business
  - **P**olitical pressures or controls
  - **T**echnological change and use of technology

- Perform a **stakeholder analysis**. Make a list of key stakeholders (as in the company profile) and then record instances of how they were treated. For example:

Employees	Scrapping of supervisory level
	Delayering of senior management
Competition	Price discrimination by post code
Customers	Good quality goods (ISO 9000)
	Good service
	Responsive to customer needs

Step 9

Now use the information you have gathered to structure your revision around the key themes you have identified. Use the exemplar questions and model answers in each chapter of this book, as well as the questions to try to help you. **Try to relate the questions to the case study you have now got for your actual exam**. This will enable you to practise the skill of **evaluation** in relation to your given scenario.

Step 10

Don't forget:

- **You will not have time in the exam to re-read the whole case study**. You must be familiar with all aspects of the scenario before your examination date.

- Pre-issued case studies are often used to examine more than one module. **Ideas and arguments from different topic areas are acceptable as Business Studies is an integrated subject.**

- To gain a high grade, **you must be able to apply your answers** to the scenario given. Therefore you need to **know your company, its history, market, production, people and product details** inside out.

- Allocate time sensibly. **Your time in the exam is for presenting your answers**, not for searching for the most appropriate quote. Copying out chunks of text will gain you few if any marks.

- Analyse past case studies for topics that have not been examined for a while. **Have you identified any of these areas as being key themes in your investigation?**

- You don't have to answer questions in the order that they are set. As long as you clearly identify on your script what question you are answering, **play to your own strengths** and the questions where you feel you have the best knowledge.

- Good evaluation considers the company's competitive position, its managerial experience and financial resources as well as the dynamic market place in which it operates. **The more detail you know, the easier your answers will become to write** and the better the grade you will get.

1 Marketing

How to score full marks

(a) Diversification is the term used when a business decides to venture into new areas. This can be in terms of either new products or new markets. By diversifying the company will have a more varied product portfolio and therefore reduce their level of risk by spreading their dependence across a range of products or markets. An example of a company that uses diversification as a tactic is Virgin, who possess a large portfolio of very different products that operate in differing market conditions.

To differentiate a product means that although there are several similar products available that perform the same function in a market, a differentiated product possesses distinct features or characteristics that separate it from other available products. An example of a market with differentiated products would be that of hi-fi equipment or video recorders where all the products perform the same basic function but possess different features.

Examiner's comment

Both terms are explained in detail, with each basic definition being expanded upon using relevant business terminology. The language is clear and unambiguous and focussed directly on the two questions being asked. An example is used in each situation to provide extra detail.

(b) For a business operating in a niche market there are several benefits that may be gained. First, a niche market usually means that the product being sold is highly differentiated or specialised in some way. This can afford the business some protection from competitors, as consumers are less likely to switch to a rival company's products because these may not meet the consumers' requirements as closely. This reduces the level of risk associated with the business.

A second benefit could be that, due to their specialist nature and the tendency of niche market consumers to be brand loyal, companies that supply products to niche markets are often able to charge a premium price. This is because niche markets are more price inelastic than markets where there is a lot of competition and this enables companies to increase their prices without a fear of losing too much demand. This can greatly benefit the company in terms of increased profit margins.

Examiner's comment

Although not a lengthy answer, the information is focussed on the question and directly relevant. The question asks for two benefits to be outlined and this has been clearly achieved by their separation into two separate paragraphs. In this type of question it can sometimes be useful to provide examples of real-life situations that will help you to further your explanations and gain top marks. However, as in the answer given, this is not always necessary.

Alongside the provision of two relevant factors, the candidate has understood that the command word 'outline' means that some development and explanation of each point is also necessary. In this case perhaps the candidate has provided a little too much development. However, it is better to over-develop your answer to achieve high levels of response, than under-develop. Just be careful that you're not spending too long on individual questions. Notice however, that it is not necessary to define the term 'niche market' to achieve full marks.

(c) **(i)** Price elasticity of demand = $\dfrac{\text{Percentage change in quantity demanded}}{\text{Percentage change in price}}$

Fall in demand is from 116 to 108 which is 8 units

so percentage change in demand = $\dfrac{8}{116} \times 100 = 6.9\%$

Rise in price from 62p to 66p which is 4 pence

so percentage change in price = $\dfrac{4}{62} \times 100 = 6.45\%$

So PED = $\dfrac{6.9}{6.45} = 1.07$ which indicates that the product is elastic.

Examiner's comment

From this response it can clearly be seen exactly what the candidate is doing at every stage of the calculation. This means that the candidate can be awarded marks as she passes through each level of the calculation: one for calculating percentage change in demand correctly, one for calculating percentage change in price and one for getting the correct answer. In this case, the student got the answer correct. However, this is always a good tactic to employ because if a mistake or error does occur, you would still be able to gain some marks for showing knowledge and understanding through your workings. If, however, no workings are shown and the answer is incorrect no marks would be awarded at all.

(ii) A market that possesses price elastic demand means that for any change in price there will be a proportionately larger change in demand. This can bring about considerable benefits for companies operating in these markets.

First, if the company reduces its prices it will see a corresponding increase in the level of demand for its products and hence it sales will rise. As demand will rise proportionally more than the decrease in price, this means that overall the company will see an increase in the level of sales revenue it receives. As the level of sales revenue increases, i.e. more sales are being made more frequently, this can help the business's cash flow position reducing the risk of liquidity problems.

Second, the company may be able to benefit from being able to price discriminate. This means that they could charge low prices to some consumers and benefit from mass-market sales and economies of scale, for example. As well as this they are able to charge a higher price to those consumers that were willing and able to pay it and thus simultaneously benefit from increased profit margins on these sales.

Examiner's comment

This is a very well-structured answer. The first paragraph contains good textbook knowledge providing a basic definition of the term and showing that the candidate has an understanding of the underlying concept. This has the effect of immediately achieving level one marks for content and/or knowledge.

In the second and third paragraphs, the candidate then expresses two relevant points. He develops them through an explanation of what each point means for the business. Benefits may be: increased sales, higher profits margins, etc.

It is easy to follow the candidate's line of reasoning as he develops each point through to a logical conclusion. This answer therefore moves through the 'levels of response' marking – content, knowledge, explanation and analysis – allowing the candidate to achieve full marks. (See page 8 for levels-of-response marking.)

There are other relevant arguments that would have served just as well as the two given. For example, a line of reasoning could have been followed that explained and developed the point that if there exist consumers who will buy the product if the price is lowered, then logically there is room for growth and expansion in this market as there are consumers who want the goods, just not at the current price.

> This is an indication of a market that is not yet saturated or one whose products are in decline and means that there exists the potential for expansion and greater sales and profits in the future.

(d) Factors that can influence the choice of distribution channel chosen by a business can vary considerably. The nature of the products supplied by Transcendental Products mean that they require no special equipment or instructions or detailed knowledge on the part of the agent or retailer who distributes the product on Transcendental's behalf. This means that a wide choice of distribution channels remain available for Helen to use as consumers need relatively little help in making their decisions about which products to purchase.

The nature of the market is also an important factor for Helen to consider though. In this case the demand for Helen's products would appear to be at national and even international level. This means that she really needs to use a chain of wholesalers or retailers to be able to satisfy the level of demand that currently exists for this type of product. At her current stage of business development, without the franchise deal it would be very difficult to Helen to supply the goods herself.

One major factor though that will influence that choice of distribution channel for any business is how much will it actually cost. An example of this is that each time a product passes through the hands of another intermediary company on its way to the consumer the final end price of that product will increase as each intermediary adds on their own profit margin. The fewer intermediaries that are used then the lower the final selling price of the product can be or the greater the profit margins that can be attained by the individual companies that are involved.

Finally the objectives of the business itself will influence the choice of channel. If, for example, the business wishes to achieve growth or an increase in market share the business will choose a channel that will allow it to retail to a mass market. Whereas, a business that wants to achieve an image of status for its products or a particular brand image, for example, may well use a more exclusive route.

In this case though, and given Helen's circumstances of facing increasing competition from mass producers and possessing price elastic products, it is my opinion that the most important factor for Transcendental Products to consider is the cost of distribution. If this is too high and Helen puts her prices up, she will lose even more sales to competitors and may be forced out of the market entirely.

Examiner's comment

This answer immediately strikes straight to core of the question. The candidate has linked his answer to the context of the question and begun the discussion of factors that do have an influence on distribution channels.

The following three paragraphs continue to discuss relevant points and develop each argument to an analytical stage by looking at cause and effect relationships, as well as the implications of various routes for differing types of situation and business.

As a final consideration the candidate has identified that evaluation requires a judgement to be made. In this case, the judgement revolves around the identification of which factor actually has the most influence on the choice of distribution channel and the candidate has selected one argument and justified, by putting it in context, why he thinks this is the most influential factor.

Note here though, that the argument selected by the candidate is not the only possible answer. It would in many circumstances be relevant to assert that the objectives of the business are the most influential factor because, if the business does not select suitable distribution channels, the business will never be able to achieve its long-term aims and it is these that provide the direction for all business decision-making.

How to score full marks

(a) (i) The term 'standard cost system' refers to a type of budgetary system used where the business determines the average or standard cost of producing a single item. The system then compares this average of how much a product should have cost with how much it actually cost to discover any differences. This then allows for monitoring and control to take place.

> **Examiner's comment**
>
> The term has been explained in detail using relevant business terminology. The question asked the candidate to explain the standard cost system, not what is a standard cost, and this has been done thoroughly. An example has not been given here but the answer includes enough information to achieve full marks despite this lack.

(ii) Cost centres are used when an organisation divides itself into areas that can be identified as having specific costs that belong to that area. The other overheads of the business are allocated to each centre on an agreed basis and each centre is run and monitored as an individual part of the business. An example of a business that might use cost centres is one that has different production lines or facilities so each one can be identified as a cost centre.

> **Examiner's comment**
>
> Again the candidate has explained this term in good depth. In fact, in both answers to part (a) the candidate has probably provided too much detail. In this case an example is used to back up the explanation. This is probably a good idea as the definition for cost centre can become muddled for many candidates.

(b) (i) Direct labour variance = Budgeted cost of labour – Actual cost of labour

where the budgeted cost = $565 \times £8.00 = £4520$

and actual cost $= 592 \times £8.40 = £4972.80$

Therefore direct labour variance = $£4520 – £4972.80 = –£452.80$

This is an adverse variance of £452.80.

(ii) Direct material variance = Budgeted cost of material – Actual cost of material

where the budgeted cost = $470 \times £3.00 = £1410$

and actual cost $= 482 \times £2.60 = £1253.20$

Therefore direct material variance = $£1410 – £1253.20 = £156.80$

This is a favourable variance of £156.80.

(iii) Profit variance = Budgeted profit – Actual profit

where profit = sales revenue – costs (fixed and variable)

So the budgeted profit = $£50\,000 – (£30\,000 + £4520 + £1410) = £14\,070$

and actual profit $= £50\,000 – (£32\,000 + £4972.80 + £1253.20) = £11\,774$

Therefore profit variance = $£14\,070 – £11\,774 = £2296$

This is an adverse variance of £2296.

(c) There are several reasons why these variances may have occurred. The adverse profit variance has arisen because of the increase in overheads as well as the adverse variances from both labour and material costs. The increase in overheads could be due to a number of factors such as an increase in rent, but realistically increases such as this should have been foreseen and budgeted for. This means there has been an unforeseen increase that could not be budgeted for in advance. This suggests that somewhere some inefficiency has crept into the business operations such as mistakes that need to be corrected which cost time and money or maybe breakdowns and repairs have increased.

The adverse labour variance could have occurred because the company has been using more labour than expected. From looking at the figures, it can be seen that they used more hours than budgeted and at a higher rate of pay than expected. As a pay rise would have been anticipated and built into the budget so a variance would not occur, this suggests that the wages have increased unexpectedly due to extra payments for either sick pay or overtime. This would also account for the extra hours that have been used because if employees have been off sick and their work needed to be covered to fulfil orders, then existing employees would have had to work longer hours on overtime rates to make up the lost production. If this is the case, it needs further investigation because an expected amount of sick time should be built into the budget for labour as well, so for this to occur there must have been a lot of people missing.

For the favourable material variance we can see that they have used more than expected, but it cost less to buy. This could be because as they have used more, they bought more, and so have benefited from discounts for bulk buying or they managed to get a cheaper supplier. One of the other possibilities is that the materials that they are using are not as good quality as previously used, so are cheaper to purchase. The lower quality of materials may also help to explain why more materials than expected were used as there might have had more waste than usual from using poorer quality materials. This would also help to explain why labour cost was adverse because if there was a lot or re-working needed due to poor quality materials then this would lead to more hours of labour being required and more overtime.

3 People and Organisations

How to score full marks

(a) Autocratic management is the term used to describe an individual manager's or a management team's approach. It implies that all decision-making powers are kept in the hands of the managers at the top of the hierarchy. Instructions flow down the levels of the organisation and employees are discouraged from giving their views or using their initiative. Managers offer no explanations and don't ask for advice on decisions that have to be made.

A paternalistic manager adopts a more father figure approach. Here the managers consult the workforce before taking decisions and explain the reasons for decisions that have been made, but still make the decisions themselves. A paternalistic manager has more consideration for the workforce and encourages a family atmosphere.

Examiner's comment

Both terms are explained in detail, with each basic definition being expanded upon using relevant business terminology. The language is clear and unambiguous and focussed directly on the question being asked. The same explanatory terms are used in each explanation to provide a clear basis for the distinction.

(b) Autocratic managers can benefit an organisation if that organisation operates in a market that faces rapid change. In this situation an autocratic manager is able to assess the situation quickly and make a rapid response. This can gain the business some competitive edge over competitors who are slower to make decisions. Furthermore, if the business is a small organisation there may not be enough competent employees to have effective delegation and consultation. In these circumstances it is beneficial to have an autocratic manager who is prepared to take control and make decisions to lead the business.

Autocratic managers do not waste as much time consulting and feeding back to subordinates. They also do not need to employ as many assistant managers because they don't delegate tasks but make all the decisions themselves. This can lead to cost savings on time not used in consensus decision-making and in the wages of middle management.

Examiner's comment

This is a good example of a clear, concise and to-the-point answer. The candidate has wasted no time with an introduction or setting the scene, but has proceeded to answer the question from the very first sentence.

Each point is stated and then developed into why this may be a benefit. Of course there are drawbacks to autocratic managers, but the question does not ask for these.

(c) To Manage by Objectives implies that the company is going to introduce a system whereby the managers and employees agree a set of objectives following consultation, discussion and negotiation. This should help both coordinate and motivate the workforce. The benefits or advantages that the company may gain are that by breaking down the aims of the company into smaller targets for individual departments or teams, or even individuals, the company can achieve a greater sense of purpose and cooperation. They can try to ensure that all employees are working in the same direction toward the same goals. This enables the firm to coordinate activities more effectively and thus make more efficient use of their resources, perhaps gaining a competitive edge as a result.

Alternatively, all employees know what they are trying to achieve and this can help as a motivator and provide enhanced feelings of satisfaction when targets are achieved. This should, according to Maslow, help to meet some employees' higher order needs. If employees are motivated they may become more productive and thus help increase efficiency. The use of consultation will improve communications throughout the business and so help reduce feelings of 'them and us', reducing the likelihood and cost of industrial actions such as go-slows, work-to-rules or, in extreme circumstances, strikes. The improved level of communications should also help managers make better decisions as they now have access to more information from the employees they consult.

On the other hand, Management by Objectives does have some problems. Just because managers consult and negotiate does not mean all parties will agree – divisive differences of opinion may occur and could be a direct cause of industrial relation problems and all the costs they incur. Similarly, the need to consult the whole workforce can lead to a very slow and costly decision-making process. If not everyone agrees on the final decision, employees are not going to take ownership of the decisions and be motivated. In fact, quite the reverse may happen. This could lead to an overall decrease in efficiency and a loss of competitive position or profits.

Examiner's comment

This is a very well-structured answer. The candidate starts by explaining the term, thus demonstrating knowledge, and goes on to examine both advantages and disadvantages as required.

In the first two paragraphs, the candidate offers several advantages. Each one is then developed in depth and linked to the first part of the question, i.e. exactly why and how these may be an advantage. The key thing to notice in these paragraphs is the way the candidate structures her answer by leading the examiner through the exact mechanics of what might happen and why this is a benefit. This is an excellent way to develop an analytical point. The candidate also introduces relevant theory at a key point and relates it well to the situation.

The third paragraph addresses the disadvantages of the system. Although not as developed as the advantages, this does not matter. The candidate has addressed both sides of the question and as such has fulfilled the examiner's requirements. Again, the style of argument is well-structured, detailing how, why and where problems might occur and the exact reasons why this would be considered a disadvantage.

(d) Increasing labour turnover could occur for many reasons. It is the underlying reason for the labour turnover that will determine the method employed to reverse the problem.

First, labour turnover may increase due to poor pay and conditions so workers leave because they are dissatisfied. This could be addressed by offering better pay rates, introducing bonus schemes, investing in a better working environment or perhaps even shortening or changing the hours of work. To determine whether or not this was the case the organisation would have to investigate what other rival firms offer employees to see if they are below standard. However, it might not be the case that employees are going to rival companies (who may be just as bad); they may be leaving the industry altogether.

Employees may therefore leave because they don't see a clear future or career path for themselves at their current company. This may be because of the organisational structure, such as a flat organisation where promotional opportunities may be few, or because the employer doesn't provide opportunities for employees to improve themselves via training or development and so move up the ladder. To solve this may involve the entire restructuring of the organisation, a very costly and time-consuming matter, or the introduction of a better human resources function that identifies employees training and development needs. This could also prove to be a costly solution and is likely to apply only to employees who are already having their basic needs (according to Maslow and Hertzberg) met.

Finally, increased labour turnover could be purely because of the management style employed, as in the case study. Employees will feel as if they have no value because they are not consulted. They are told what to do and have no chance to use their own initiative or develop ideas. The manager does not delegate responsibility and so the tasks employees are given to do are likely to be boring and monotonous, thus causing de-motivation and high labour turnover. This could be avoided by providing a more democratic or even paternalistic management approach or by adopting a programme of job enrichment and enlargement to provide employees with more tasks and responsibility. However, it will again take time to implement these changes and it may not be possible to change a management style without changing the manager, as in the question. For some businesses where the owner is also the manager this really is not a viable option.

In conclusion, the way a business responds to an increase in labour turnover is dependent on a number of factors: the cause of the labour turnover, how much it is going to cost to implement any changes and whether the business can afford them, the length of time and scale of changes involved as well as the type of ownership of the firm. In the case of Fairchild's Motors, the solution appears to be changing management style.

Examiner's comment

This answer starts with an evaluative statement. The candidate then proceeds to develop analytical points as to why increasing labour turnover might arise and how to combat it.

She discusses a number of relevant points and develops each argument to an analytical stage by looking at cause-and-effect relationships, as well as the implications of various solutions for the specific business.

The candidate weighs up the possible pros and cons of each solution as she goes through her answer as required for evaluation. The introduction of relevant theory in the third paragraph is appropriate.

The candidate concludes by stating what she thinks are the dependent factors that would have a major influence on the actual solution implemented and so places her answer in context.

How to score full marks

(a) The term 'benchmarking' refers to the situation when one business sets itself performance targets based on the achievements of the most efficient organisation in the industry. This then focusses the attention of managers and employees on achievements that are possible and then need to be attained to become more competitive in the market.

> **Examiner's comment**
>
> This is a well-written and fluid explanation. It can be difficult to explain or define some business terms. It therefore often pays to learn some of the ones you may find trickier.

(b) Holding high levels of stock could mean that the business is incurring unnecessary costs. Holding stock means that the business needs to have space available to do so. This is unproductive space that incurs costs such as rent and rates or insurance for the premises and also for the stock, whilst at the same time earns no revenue. The business will also need to employ staff to handle and secure the stock – again incurring increased costs in the form of wages.

There is also an associated opportunity cost in holding stock – that money tied up in stocks cannot be used elsewhere. This restricts the amount of working capital that is available to the business, which could cause liquidity problems. Alternatively, it could be used in other investments such as training or better production facilities or working conditions. These would all have the ability of actually being able to generate some returns for the business either through increased production or motivation.

> **Examiner's comment**
>
> The question asks for two benefits to be outlined and this has been clearly achieved and is easily identifiable by their separation into two separate paragraphs. The information is focussed on the question and directly relevant.
>
> The candidate has understood that the command word 'outline' means that some development and explanation of each point is also necessary. In this case perhaps the candidate has provided a little too much development. However, it is better to over-develop your answer to achieve high levels of response, rather than under-develop. Just be careful that you are not spending too long on individual questions. This candidate has not wasted a lot of time on needless introductory statements.

(c) (i) A quality circle is a group of employees that meet in order to solve quality problems. The idea is that the members of the circle should have different expertise so that they are able to fully discuss quality problems and come up with workable solutions. These are typically used in motor manufacturers such as Toyota.

> **Examiner's comment**
>
> Again, a good, clear and to-the-point explanation. The candidate has used a good example (in fact, Toyota introduced the idea of quality circles) and has made the purpose and the make-up of a quality circle evident. The only addition here could have been the fact that quality circles make suggestions for solutions, they don't implement them and, as such, are a useful form of consultation.

(ii) The use of Kaizen or continuous improvement can bring many benefits to a business. First, and perhaps foremost, is that it should help improve the business's competitive position. This is because Kaizen looks at making lots of small improvements throughout the business. For example, a production worker may look at small ways of making products more quickly whereas the distribution manager may try to find cheaper, more cost effective delivery systems or routes. All these small improvements eventually add to the business being able to produce and sell goods more efficiently and effectively, thus helping to improve either its competitive position through prices or improve its profit margins.

Secondly, the business should be able to experience these benefits without large-scale resistance from workers. This is because, initially, the workers may have made a suggestion themselves so that, if and when it is used, they are going to feel happy and motivated. This agrees with motivational theorists who suggest that recognition helps build employees' self-esteem and motivation levels. This, in turn, raises productivity because motivated workers are more productive as they take less time off and they are also more willing to make suggestions for improvements in the future, thus improving the whole system.

Finally, as the focus is on small changes no changes should be major enough to cause large-scale discontent or disruption anyway. This then enables the business to implement changes and improvements to production without the fear of worker retaliation or industrial action. Again, this allows them to improve productive efficiency and their competitive position without disruption to the production process.

Examiner's comment

This is very good and well-structured answer. The first paragraph contains good textbook knowledge and explanatory examples. The candidate has shown an understanding of the underlying concept. This has the effect of immediately achieving marks for application and the final part of the paragraph introduces some analysis with the development of the cause/effect relationship.

In the second and third paragraphs the candidate then expresses two relevant points and develops them through an explanation of what each point means, to an analysis of the cause/effect or implication.

It would have been good if the candidate had related to specific motivational theorists such as Hertzberg or, perhaps, Maslow.

(d) The introduction of a JIT manufacturing system could have many advantages and disadvantages to a company like Aldred's. First I will look at the advantages that could be gained.

Through the use of a JIT stock system they will no longer require the warehousing space that they previously did. This then could be turned into increased production space improving overall capacity and perhaps increasing the economies of scale experienced by the business. At the very least, the business should experience a reduction in costs, as they will no longer have the costs of stockholding to fund. If possible, and this depends on whether or not the warehouse facilities were a separate building, they could perhaps sell or lease this building to someone else and thus receive a cash injection into the business.

Furthermore, JIT focusses on reducing waste by removing or cutting back on non-value-adding activities within the production process. This may mean that the business will incur lower costs. If products aren't left hanging around for long periods of time between one production process and the next, they may even be produced faster. This could mean increased capacity or more sales as products can reach the customer quicker, again meaning more profits for Aldred's.

However, in order to do this, the system needs to be implemented in the first place. This will initially increase the costs of the business a great deal. First they will need new systems for ordering and receiving stock on a JIT basis. Then all the staff will require training on how and what they are now meant to do. This will be very expensive, not only in terms of the training itself, but also due to lost production as staff attend training events. The difficulty here is that the business needs to spend the money on all these aspects a long time before they can expect to see major benefits. This may cause problems with cash flow and working capital.

In my opinion, the benefits that could be gained outweigh the costs involved. However, whether or not this is suitable for Aldred's depends on several factors. First, whether they actually have the money to invest in new techniques. Given their current position, borrowing money may well be out of the question and increased payments from interest charges would only increase the strain on working capital even more. Second, JIT stock control is entirely dependent on the reliability of suppliers. For a toy manufacturer demand should be fairly easy to predict – peaks at Christmas and such – but if they can't find the suppliers then they can't implement the system. Finally, Aldred's should be able to find areas of the production process where waste activities can be cut back and benefits gained, so these areas should definitely be pursued. Resistance from employees should be small as Lee is discussing the situation with them and they all know that without some improvements, none of them will have a job.

Examiner's comment

The introductory paragraph contains no content, but many candidates do find this a useful technique for focussing their answer on the question.

The candidate provides a balanced argument on the pros and cons of JIT manufacture. This is perhaps slightly more biased towards advantages, but this does not cause concern as he does consider both sides of the question.

Each point is developed fully by analysing why it would be considered an advantage or disadvantage, by stating the factor to be considered, explaining what might take place and highlighting the knock-on effects of this to the business. The candidate also makes some preliminary evaluative statements by considering the timescale differences between the costs and benefits.

The final evaluation sums up the important factors and makes judgements about the difficulties or likelihood of events occurring. The key factor here is that the candidate makes a distinction between JIT stock control and JIT systems used in production and delivers a viable judgement based on logical reasoning.

---

5 External Influences

How to score full marks

1   (a) Business ethics are the written or unwritten moral code which dictates how a business behaves. They are the underlying code of honour that influence what decisions a business should and should not take. An example would be 'Should an employer accept a profitable contract even if it knew that it would damage the environment?'

   (b) A pressure group is an organisation of people who support a common cause and act in unison to support or promote that cause to others. An example of pressure group could be ASH whose aim is to try and promote anti-smoking activities.

Examiner's comment

These are both concise, clear and to-the-point definitions. The candidate uses good terminology and supports both definitions with suitable examples. In part (a) the candidate has used an example not given in the case study text. This avoids the problem of just re-wording information already provided.

2   The first course of action a business may take is to do nothing. They may consider the actions of the pressure group to be of no particular concern – the pressure group is too small or not powerful enough to generate any media interest. The company may therefore decide that as any effects are likely to be minuscule it is not sufficiently cost effective to warrant any action.

Alternatively, the company could fight back against the pressure group by undertaking a public relations campaign to try to offset any damage the pressure group may cause. As another option, depending on the actions of the pressure group, the business could instigate legal actions for libel, slander or perhaps even damaging property.

Examiner's comment

The question asks for two courses of action to be explained. This has been done clearly and is easily identifiable by their separation into two paragraphs. In fact, the candidate has offered three possible responses whereas two would have been enough.

An interesting point is that a possible course of action in any situation is to do nothing. If you use this argument, you would need to back it up with a rationale of why this might be a suitable course of action.

The candidate has understood that the command word 'explain' means that some development and explanation of each point is also necessary. In this case, the candidate has offered more points than necessary. However, the concise writing style means that not too much time has been wasted.

---

3   The government could have helped Smith's with their negotiations in several ways. Firstly, the Government would probably have assisted Smith's by providing information about the size and nature of their potential customer. This is similar to market research information and would have saved Smith's the cost of having to find out the information for themselves. This actually makes the cost of negotiating contracts a lot cheaper. Alongside this, Smith's would have been able to structure their negotiation strategy to target their efforts towards the client's needs, thus gaining them an advantage over competing companies from different countries.

Alternatively, the Government often helps to promote British businesses overseas by arranging trade fairs and exhibitions. It also assists with travel costs and promotional costs for some companies who are conducting international negotiations. This again would have helped Smith's keep the cost of negotiations down, and so enabled them to stay in the running for the contract longer or perhaps enabled them to start negotiations in the first place. This gives British business a huge 'helping hand' as this type of contract negotiation can often be lengthy and very costly.

Finally, the Government may have helped by acting as a referee or guarantor. It says in the text that the UK Government use Smith's products themselves. This could greatly enhance Smith's reputation with an overseas government and help them to secure the sale. Alternatively, the British Government may have exerted some pressure on the foreign government in return for past or future trade concessions.

Examiner's comment

A good, clear and to-the-point explanation. The candidate has shown a good understanding of how international negotiations can and do take place. He has placed his answer in the context of the question and used the text from the case study to help support his answer. This is not the same as just re-wording or copying out the text. In this case, the candidate has used it as part of a relevant argument.

---

4   There are several methods that the Government could use to try and control the level or extent of environmental damage caused by Smith's building of their new factory. Firstly, they could use direct legislative measures. The Environmental Protection Act sets upper boundaries on the amounts of pollution that manufacturing sites are allowed to produce. The Government could monitor Smith's activities and, if they are found to be contravening the Act, can impose substantial fines upon Smith's. In extreme cases, if Smith's were found to be contravening the law and did so persistently, the Government could even force the closure of the factory. This threat of fines or potential closure could therefore force Smith's themselves to controlling the level of environmental damage.

Alternatively, the Government could require Smith's to pay compensation to the residents of Harford if it could be proved that Smith's were causing damage to the community environment. For example, the residents have voiced noise pollution as one of their concerns. The Government could order Smith's to pay compensation to those residents within a certain distance for whom noise levels would be disturbing. This compensation may go some way to compensating the community. The Government could advise that such compensation levels would be so high that Smith's undertake to reduce the amount of noise or other pollution their factory emits. This would then remove the need for them to pay any compensation at all and perhaps be the cheaper alternative in the long run.

Finally, the Government could, as a last resort, impose a tax on the amount of pollution caused by Smith's. These funds could be used to offset the effects of the pollution. This doesn't actually control the amount of pollution generated – it just acts as a method whereby the Government can raise funds so it can afford to clean up and remove the pollution later. A drawback of this method is that the funds collected would go to help pollution nationwide, not directly to the residents of Harford.

As a possible measure, the Government or EU authorities could offer to help Smith's by giving them grants to invest in more expensive but perhaps less environmentally damaging production methods. However, these really won't help the fact that the factory will still be built.

5 By operating an ethical business policy Smith's profits could be greatly improved. Because of the nature of the market they operate in, some aspects of ethical business may be difficult for them to achieve. However, this does not mean that they cannot act in an ethical manner at all. They are still able to act in a morally correct way toward their employees, customers and other stakeholders. Being perceived as a company that does act in a morally correct way, given their chosen field of operations, may actually be a huge benefit in attracting customers. This is because Smith's will be perceived as a company that can be relied upon and trusted and so may help Smith's gain sales. This would hopefully result in increased profits.

Similarly, many employees may be trained in this type of manufacturing or this particular industry. They may well feel that that they would rather work for a company that has some ethical policies and responsibilities, rather than for one that doesn't. This means that comparatively speaking Smith's may well be able to recruit better qualified, more conscientious and highly motivated workers. In the long run this would result in increased profitability through increased productive efficiency and associated cost savings.

However, there is a negative side for Smith's as well. They may have to turn down very profitable contracts from other governments or countries if they regard them to be outside the limits of their ethical policy. The text does not state the name of the country they are dealing with. However, it would be hoped in this context that, even a military vehicles manufacturer with an ethical policy would turn down contracts from countries with poor human rights records, no matter how lucrative. This would result in a loss in potential profitability, but may gain them customers elsewhere.

They could incur increased costs as a lot of time and money would be spent debating which decisions were or were not ethical, especially given this company's circumstances. In this context a lot of resources could be wasted in lengthy debate about whether or not any particular decision should be undertaken. This again would reduce the potential profitability of the business. Instead of being tied up in time-consuming discussions, management could spend their time more usefully in generating sales, solving production problems or improving production processes or quality, for example. This would be a much more effective way of generating profits.

> **Examiner's comment**
>
> This is a very good answer to a difficult question. When it comes to questions about ethics, candidates often find it impossible to keep their own opinions and beliefs to themselves and discuss the answer in a rational manner.
>
> Despite the obviously tricky nature of the business in which Smith's operate, they have realised that while Smith's may not be the most ethical business ever encountered, it is still possible for them to behave in an ethical manner for their particular industry. Whether or not the candidate agrees is irrelevant. This candidate has therefore developed a good analytical answer discussing both sides of the argument and putting it in the context of the question. Again, an obvious structure of separate paragraphs for separate points helps the examiner follow the development of each point.

6 Whether or not businesses should operate in a more environmentally friendly way is matter for considerable debate.

Firstly, one of the problems with being environmentally friendly is that it usually means increased costs for the business. This could be due to the purchase and implementation of new 'greener' machinery, training for employees to become more environmentally aware or having to use sustainable energy sources or material sources. Obviously, for example, harvesting and replanting is going to be more expensive than harvesting alone. These may well have to be absorbed by the business in the form of lower profit margins. Alternatively, they could raise the prices but this will inevitably lead to a fall in demand for their products.

Secondly, being environmentally friendly may place you at a competitive disadvantage to competitors who are not. Overseas producers for example, especially if from less developed countries often don't have to comply with the same environmental legislation as do UK companies. This means that they can produce goods much more cheaply and so gain a price advantage and undercut western producers to generate sales.

However, being environmentally friendly and holding awards such as BS7750 can help a company gain clients. Businesses can win major contracts from other like-minded companies – if you don't hold this certificate you can't even bid for some contracts. Consumers are also likely to be impressed by the image of environmentally friendly companies and so are more willing to purchase their products, thus increasing sales and profits for the company.

Whether or not a company is actually environmentally friendly, I think, depends on several factors. Firstly, the size of the company – small companies are not likely to attract the attention of pressure groups or the media. They can be environmentally friendly or not, but few people would notice anyway so why have increased costs? Secondly, the sector of the economy in which the business operates – it would probably be advisable for primary industries involved in agriculture to be fairly environmentally friendly. However, if you were a secondary manufacturer of tablemats, would anybody really care? However, tertiary companies that deal directly with the general public probably have more need to be environmentally friendly. As a final point, it also depends on the product's price elasticity. If the product is price inelastic then the business can be environmentally friendly as they can pass the costs onto the consumer.

> **Examiner's comment**
>
> The candidate here has written a rather long-winded discussion of the question but has raised valid points throughout and reached a reasoned judgement.
>
> The first two paragraphs consider the cons side of environmental issues, and discuss the problems that a company may encounter and the results this may have on their competitive position and price.
>
> The third paragraph looks at the other side of the argument and considers how a business might benefit. All four paragraphs develop points in logical sequences, moving through skills and levels of response.
>
> The final evaluative paragraph is in-depth and well-reasoned, and offers three separate points as to why or why not business would want to be environmentally friendly.
>
> A criticism that could be levelled at this answer is that it is far too long. The candidate could have constructed the same arguments in approximately half the space.

6 Objectives and Strategy

How to score full marks

1 **(a)** The term 'Ltd' means that the company is a private limited company. It is a limited liability company that operates in the private sector and that has shareholders. However, the shares are not dealt on the stock exchange and are not available to the general public

(b) The exchange rate is the value of the domestic currency in relation to the relative value of other currencies. It is the value of sterling compared to the currency of another country and the exchange rate is the current ratio at which the two currencies are traded.

2   A fall in the rate of interest could affect J & M Taylor in several ways. Firstly, the fall in interest levels would cause consumers to have higher levels of disposable income. This is because interest payments on loans or mortgages should fall. This implies that consumers would have more spending power and demand in the economy would rise. This would mean increased expenditure on take-away food and hence greater sales for Taylor's as their clients order more supplies to fulfil increased customer demand.

Secondly, it is possible that Taylor's themselves have outstanding loans or mortgages, especially as they've only been established 20 years (mortgages are generally 25 years long). This means that they too could benefit in a reduction in interest payment, causing a decrease in the business overheads and a rise in profits.

3   The main stakeholders who would be affected by this decision are the employees and their unions, shareholders and the local community.

At the announcement of possible job cuts, employees will start to lose job security – that their own jobs are safe. According to the Maslow's hierarchy of needs, security is one of the lower order motivators and so, if removed, would cause a drop in worker motivation. This outcome is supported by Hertzberg who classified job security as a hygiene factor whose removal would cause dissatisfaction amongst the workforce. The loss of motivation would cause workers to react by decreasing productivity levels or perhaps manifest itself as increased absenteeism. It is also likely that the unions would wish to intervene on their employees' behalf and negotiate with management in an attempt to save jobs. They may react by offering the management reduced hours per employee, or even a small cut in pay in order to save jobs.

The local community would probably fear that there would be increased unemployment and fewer prospects. There may also be fears of rising crime and a local economic downturn as the redundancies of many local workers would also have knock-on effects to other local businesses whose turnover and profits are reliant on the workers spending their wages. In this respect it is likely that local residents would campaign for jobs to be saved, either directly to the business or via their local MP.

The shareholders of the business would probably fear that a reduction in employment would mean falling output levels, a corresponding rise in costs per unit as fixed costs are spread out over fewer units of production, and hence a squeeze in profit margins. It is unlikely that any higher costs could be passed to consumers as this, no doubt, would cause a further fall in demand and sales, and consequently more job losses. If shareholders fear falling profits and hence dividend levels, they may seek to sell their shares and place the investment elsewhere. In the context of the question, this is unlikely as it is a private limited family-owned business.

4 (a)

Strengths	Weaknesses
The major strength of the business is that they have been established for over twenty years. This means that they have experience in the industry and likely to have suffered from fluctuation in demand before. This can provide invaluable expertise into how best to weather the storm. Furthermore, after twenty years, the company may well have a considerable base of fixed assets to fall back on or retained profit reserves built up over time.	One of their major problems with two of the current plans is that there is no indication that Taylor's have any experience at all in retailing or exporting operations. This could lead them into taking major risks without perhaps the necessary knowledge or resources to be able to proceed with much chance of success. Alongside this, their current order book is falling – meaning than any risky operations are unlikely to be supported by current sales levels while they take time to get established.
Opportunities	**Threats**
Taylor's appear to have spotted a gap in the market for a niche take-away food outlet. As this is a niche market with no local competition Taylor's would be able to take advantage of charging a premium price. This would raise profit levels and, as organic food is currently fashionable, there may well be effective demand in place.	The major threat to Taylor's operation at the moment would appear to be the fact that demand and sales are falling. The text highlights the point that local people are economising and unemployment is rising. It is therefore unlikely that, even with falling exchange rates, sales will pick up soon.

(b) Out of the three options available I think that the most risky and least likely to succeed is the proposal to start exporting. Firstly, as already outlined, Taylor's have absolutely no experience in this line of business. This means that they would either have to trust to their instincts – a very risky option when considering fluctuating exchange rates – or invest a lot of money in terms of gaining advice, contacts and expertise. My main argument for not favouring this proposal is that Taylor's deal in perishable food items and unless they receive a huge amount of orders from one place their delivery costs are going to be very high. The case study does not mention to which countries they would export, but from the North East of England to any countries farther away than Norway, Sweden, etc. or France transport costs would be huge, as the goods would need specialised refrigeration equipment to transport them so they arrive fresh. This is a reasonable cost for bulk carriers to assume but not, in my opinion, a small company like Taylor's.

The second idea of the organic food outlet I think is a fairly good one. Although I believe their lack of experience in this area is risky as well. What makes Taylor's think they can succeed in a market full of experienced establishments that are facing declining sales? I therefore think their lack of experience is a key problem. Alongside this, to my knowledge, you cannot patent or copyright a sandwich. Therefore, if this idea did succeed, it would be very short-lived, as all the other outlets would start to copy them. Although a market may be present, it is a niche market and therefore unlikely that there are enough organic food consumers to support every local fast food outlet. It is my opinion that this option would also be very risky and any benefits short-lived.

I also don't think reducing the workforce is a very good idea either. Problems associated with falling motivation levels and productivity are almost bound to occur even if Taylor's consult and communicate with their workforce and unions throughout the entire process. At a time when pressure is being put on profits and sales I don't think heavy redundancy payments or the risk of rising costs through decreased productivity and maybe industrial action is worth it.

In my opinion, Taylor's should communicate the problem of falling sales and dropping profits to the workforce. With large-scale job losses elsewhere it will hardly come as a surprise to them. Then I think Taylor's should remind the workforce of their twenty years of success and inform them that Taylor's intends to survive with their help. I believe that if Taylor's communicate well with their workforce and offer them all safe jobs but on reduced shifts or hours, thus saving costs and reducing capacity, there should not be any loss in productivity through de-motivation. In fact, through a consultation and communication process the reverse may happen. If there is any resistance Taylor's could highlight the fact that they imagine the current situation to be short term due to the fall in interest rates, which should hopefully start to stimulate demand again. If the situation does deteriorate further they could perhaps lose staff through natural wastage or ask for volunteers or early retirements to take place.

Examiner's comment

This is a very good answer to a difficult question. When it comes to questions requiring judgements and recommendation students often struggle to express themselves clearly. They frequently rely on assertion or statements that something is so without using logical reasoning to establish it. This would score only low-level evaluation marks.

Each possible proposal is discussed as a separate item, and the basis for whether or not to proceed discussed in a well-structured manner. The interesting thing about this response, and why it has been chosen for this text, is that the candidate has chosen not to recommend any of the proposals but instead elected for an idea of his own. This is a perfectly reasonable approach to take provided, as this candidate has done, the reasoning behind the judgement and recommendation is fully developed and justified.

5 An upturn in the business cycle would tend to indicate that the economy is coming out of a slump. This would have several effects for a business such as Taylor's.

Firstly, an upturn would indicate that GDP is starting to rise – that output is starting to increase. If this happens then employment will also rise as companies will need more employees to fuel the increased output levels. More people in employment indicates that there will be increased demand in the economy as these people now have higher disposable incomes. This would tend to indicate an increase in sales of take-away food and hence an opportunity to increase sales volume and profits for Taylor's as well.

The increase in demand may indicate that it could be time for Taylor's to expand their productive capacity, especially if economic indicators highlight a probable boom is on the way. The difficulty here though is that with increased employment, potential employees may be scarce and so demand higher wages, thus increasing business cost and squeezing profit margins. Taylor's may be able to pass some of these cost increases on to customers in the form of higher prices, but this is unlikely as in a competitive industry – Taylor's products are likely to be price elastic. It is also likely that, given the high current rate of unemployment, for a reasonable period of time Taylor's should still be able to recruit employees without much trouble or higher wage demands. Thus they could take the opportunity to increase productive capacity by hiring extra employees.

Taylor's may use a period of increased demand to undertake some investment projects such as newer machinery or training for employees. This would enable them to improve their productive efficiency, and also motivation if training was utilised. So Taylor's would be able to increase their productive capacity and benefit from increased economies of scale – in this case, technical economies from better machinery.

Other opportunities that exist in a possible future upturn in the business environment is that, perhaps with increasing sales revenue, cash flow and profits, Taylor's may now be able to undertake one of the options of opening a retail outlet or expanding abroad. The arguments for their lack of expertise still exist, but with increased activity on the traditional business this reduces the financial risk of undertaking these proposals. It also increases the opportunities for obtaining investment funds, as the upturn may well have been stimulated by falling interest rates, thus reducing the cost of borrowing.

It is my opinion that as take-away food is an income-elastic product, sales for take-away food will increase and so therefore will Taylor's orders. Taylor's should take advantage of this to increase their current capacity to match increasing levels of demand in an area where they have experience and expertise. It may not be feasible for Taylor's to expand their current premises or move to another site due to cost factors or lack of availability of suitable locations. However, their productive capacity and efficiency could be increased by investment in better machinery and training for employees. This is also a less risky option and, if the upturn proves to be short lived, can be scaled down without the major costs of discontinuing operations.

Examiner's comment

The candidate here has produced an in-depth response to the question and, has raised valid points throughout to come to a weighted conclusion as to what he feels the most likely and best opportunity for J & M Taylor's would be.

Each paragraph considers a separate opportunity. Although paragraphs two and three discuss a similar opportunity, the methods of achieving it – the cause-and-effect relationship – are different, so these count as separate lines of reasoning.

Notice that the candidate offers evaluation throughout this answer, not just in the final paragraph. The likelihood of finding employees and the possibilities of obtaining investment funds are both examples of evaluative statements. Finally, the candidate determines that the deciding factors are degree of risk, in terms of financial risk, level of expertise possessed in different situations and the possibility of timescale. This justifies top-level marks for fully justified evaluation.